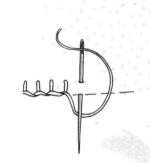

And Sew to Bed

And Sew to Bed

VANESSA MOONCIE

GUILD OF MASTER CRAFTSMAN PUBLICATIONS

First published 2013 by
Guild of Master Craftsman Publications Ltd
Castle Place, 166 High Street, Lewes,
East Sussex BN7 1XU

ISBN 978 1 86108 889 5

A catalogue record for this book is available
from the British Library.

Publisher Jonathan Bailey
Production Manager Jim Bulley
Managing Editor Gerrie Purcell
Senior Project Editor Dominique Page
Editor Sarah Hoggett
Managing Art Editor Gilda Pacitti
Designer Rebecca Mothersole
Still-life photography Holly Joliffe
Fashion photography Sian Irvine
Model Joelle Coutinho at MOT Models
Hair and make-up Jeni Dodson

Set in Avenir
Colour origination by GMC Reprographics

Printed and bound in China

For my mum,
who taught me to sew

Contents

Introduction

Popularity for vintage style is as strong as ever, with past designs being recreated and reinvented in the fashion houses and on the high street year upon year. Designers take their inspiration from the elegant gowns and loungewear of the 1920s and 30s; the evening clothes and practical daywear of the 1940s; and the classic, tailored suits and dresses, emphasizing the hourglass figure, of the 1950s. An original vintage piece will guarantee an individual style of good quality, which has often been produced in small quantities and is therefore far removed from the mass-produced look.

The inspiration for this book stems from the Hollywood glamour and Art-Deco style of the 1920s and 30s and moves through to the chic New Look of the post-war years, with its make-do-and-mend mentality, unlike the throw-away attitude seen in recent times.

The Second World War brought about a resurgence in home sewing with women creating new from old, remodelling garments to refresh and update their wardrobe and sewing for the war effort. In the 1950s, although sewing dwindled as the economy became more prosperous, Hollywood was a great source of inspiration, with women copying the looks at home with the aid of designer sewing patterns, which had become available. Nowadays, with the emphasis on looking after the environment, together with the thrill of finding a pretty vintage fabric that can be transformed with a little imagination, more of us are again sewing for ourselves, our families and our homes.

This book contains 20 projects that will add a beautiful vintage touch to your bedroom and wardrobe, all explained with easy-to-follow, illustrated step-by-step instructions. The designs are aimed at all abilities, ranging from small and simple items, such as the lavender bag and powder puff, to a more challenging dressing gown and pleated lampshade. The section at the back of the book on honing your skills will equip you with everything you need to know to create each piece. The aim is to build confidence in beginners and inspire those of you who are more experienced in needlework, so that by working through all the projects, you will not only be furnishing your boudoir, you will also be gaining that great sense of personal satisfaction that can be achieved by sewing a garment or article for your home.

CREATE
THE LOOK

Nº 1

Powder Puff

The large, fluffy puff is ideal for pampering
yourself with a dusting of powder to the neck
and shoulders. Use the smaller size in a soft
velvet fabric to apply your make-up.

FABRIC REQUIRED

LARGE POWDER PUFF

Without satin base	16 x 8in (40 x 20cm)
With satin base	8 x 8in (20 x 20cm) each in main fabric and satin

SMALL POWDER PUFF

Without satin base	8 x 4in (20 x 10cm)
With satin base	4 x 4in (10 x 10cm) each in main fabric and satin

SUGGESTED FABRICS Good-quality fur fabric or velvet; stretch fabrics are not suitable

SEWING NOTIONS
* Thread to match fabric
* Small amount of toy stuffing

For the large powder puff
* Two 15in (38cm) lengths of satin ribbon, 1in (2.5cm) wide

For the small powder puff
* Two 9in (23cm) lengths of satin ribbon, ¼in (6mm) wide

FINISHED SIZES
Large powder puff:
6¾in (17cm) across
Small powder puff:
2½in (6cm) across

SEAM ALLOWANCES
Take ⅝in (1.5cm) seam allowances throughout unless otherwise stated

KEY
wrong side of fabric
right side of fabric

'I don't mind living
in a man's world as long
as I can be a woman in it.'

MARILYN MONROE

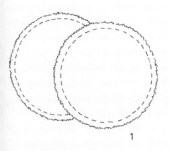

1

Enlarge the patterns on page 170 by 300% and cut out. Cut one circle each for the top and base of the powder puff in your chosen fabric. Staystitch (see page 152) around each piece, ⅛in (3mm) from the outside edge.

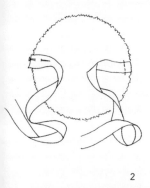

2

Place one circle right side up. Pin one ribbon on each side, as indicated by the dots on the pattern. Tack in place.

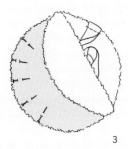

3

3 Making sure that the ribbons are sandwiched in the centre of the two circles and tucked right away from the edges, place both pieces of fabric with right sides together and pin. The direction of the pile is not too important, but it looks neater if it lays the same way on both sides of the powder puff.

4

4 Stitch the pieces together, leaving a small opening of about 1½–2in (4–5cm) for the small powder puff and 3in (7.5cm) for the large. Trim the seam and notch the curves (see page 147).

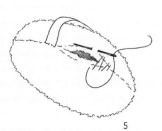

5

5 Turn the powder puff right side out and fill with stuffing to form a padded shape. Be careful not to overstuff or your powder puff won't feel so light to the touch. Turn under the seam of the opening and close with a ladder stitch (see page 152).

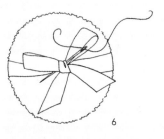

6

6 Use a blunt-ended needle to tease out the pile that has been caught in the stitches at the seams. Tie a bow with the ribbon in the centre of the powder puff and secure the knot with a few hidden stitches by hand. Trim the ends of the ribbon to finish.

Nightdress

The fabric that you choose for this nightdress
can transform the way it looks: a floral cotton
lawn will create a simple, cosy look, while a
lightweight silk will add a glamorous quality.

PATTERN PIECES

1 FRONT YOKE
2 BACK YOKE
3 BACK
   (JOIN 3A + 3B)
4 FRONT
   (JOIN 4A + 4B)

FABRIC REQUIRED

To calculate the length of fabric you need, refer to the appropriate column for your dress size and the fabric width you are using.

FABRIC WIDTH	SMALL	MEDIUM	LARGE
36in (90cm) without nap	2⅜yd (2.2m)	n/a	n/a
45in (115cm) without nap	2⅜yd (2.2m)	2½yd (2.3m)	2½yd (2.3m)
60in (150cm) without nap	2yd (1.8m)	2⅛yd (1.95m)	2⅛yd (1.95m)

SUGGESTED FABRICS Broderie anglaise, cotton lawn, voile, silk charmeuse, silk taffeta

SEWING NOTIONS

* Thread to match fabric
* 25in (64cm) satin ribbon, around ¾in (2cm) wide
* 1yd (90cm) bias binding, ½in (12mm) wide

SEAM ALLOWANCES

Take ⅝in (1.5cm) seam allowances throughout, unless otherwise stated

FINISHED SIZE

Back length from shoulder
Small: 37in (93.5cm)
Medium: 38½in (97.5cm)
Large: 40in (101.5cm)

Width around hem
Small: 65¾in (167cm)
Medium: 69½in (176.5cm)
Large: 76½in (186.5cm)

KEY

wrong side of fabric
right side of fabric

36IN (90CM) SMALL SIZE ONLY
45IN (115CM) ALL SIZES

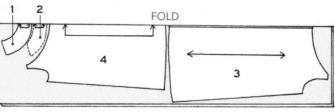

60IN (150CM)
ALL SIZES

BROKEN LINES INDICATE
REVERSE SIDE OF PATTERNS

Front and back yokes

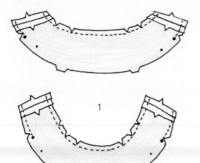

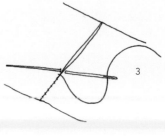

1 Turn under ⅝in (1.5cm) at the shoulder edges of both the back and front yoke facings and press (see page 157). With right sides together, matching the notches, small dots and large dots, pin the facings and yoke pieces together. Stitch the neck edge and from the shoulders to the large dots. Trim the seams and clip the curves (see page 147).

2 Turn the yokes right side out and press. With right sides together, taking care not to catch the facings in the stitches, stitch the shoulder seam of the front and back yokes.

3 Tuck the shoulder seam inside the facing and slipstitch (see page 151) the edges together.

Back and front

4 With right sides together, matching the notches, pin and stitch the centre back seam.

5 Pin the front and back right sides together, matching the notches, and stitch the side seams. Press the seams open. Turn the nightdress right side out.

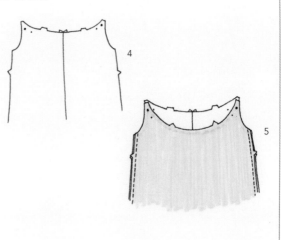

Armholes

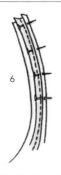

6 Open out one edge of the bias binding and, with right sides together, pin the crease line of the binding to the seam line of the armhole. Stitch in place along the crease.

7 Trim the seam and press the bias binding to the inside of the armhole. Slipstitch the binding in place on the inside of the armhole.

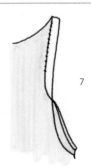

Attaching yoke

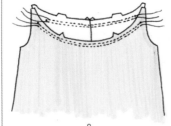

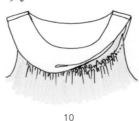

8 Run two rows of gathering stitches (see page 155) in between the small dots on the front and back garment pieces, by hand or using a long machine stitch, working one row along the seam line and the other ¼in (6mm) inside the seam line.

9 Press under ⅝in (1.5cm) around the lower edge of the yoke facing.

10 With right sides together, matching the notches, small dots and large dots, pin the yoke to the front and back pieces. Gather the main pieces evenly to fit the yoke and stitch in place.

11 Press the seam up so that it lies between the yoke and the facing. Pin and slipstitch the yoke facing in place on the inside, matching notches and small dots.

Finishing off

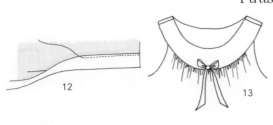

12 Turn under 1in (2.5cm) at the hem and press. Turn the raw edge under and press, then stitch the hem.

13 Tie the ribbon into a bow and sew to the centre front of the yoke. Trim the ends of the ribbon at an angle.

Lavender Bag

By using small vintage embroidered finds,
each little bag will be unique and would make
the perfect gift to scent a drawer or wardrobe,
as well as looking pretty.

FABRIC REQUIRED

7 x 6in (18 x 15cm) main fabric
7 x 6in (18 x 15cm) lining fabric (if required)

SUGGESTED FABRICS Embroidered linens or handkerchiefs in cotton, linen or silk

SEWING NOTIONS

* Thread to match fabric
* 7in (18cm) lace, ⅜–2in (1–5cm) wide
* Around 12in (30.5cm) ribbon, ⅛–⅞in (3mm–2cm) wide
* Dried lavender to fill bag

FINISHED SIZE

5⅜in (13.5cm) high x 3⅛in (8cm) wide

KEY

wrong side of fabric
right side of fabric

SEAM ALLOWANCES

Take ⅜in (1cm) seam allowances throughout, unless otherwise stated

1   Cut an oblong of fabric to the required size: mine was 7 x 6in (18 x 15cm), but you can make the bag smaller or larger simply by increasing or reducing these measurements. If your fabric has cutwork or lacy inserts, place a layer of lining fabric, cut to the same size, behind it, to avoid losing the lavender filling.

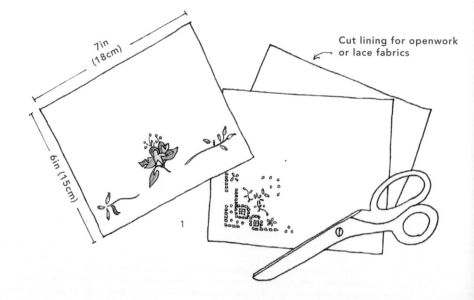

7in (18cm)

6in (15cm)

Cut lining for openwork or lace fabrics

1

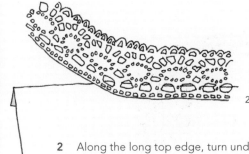

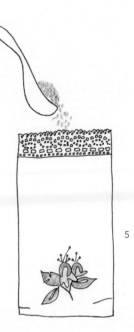

2 Along the long top edge, turn under a ¼in (6mm) hem and press (see page 157). Pin the lace to the front of the work across the pressed edge and stitch in place.

5 Turn the work right side out and carefully push out the corners with a knitting needle or the tip of a pencil. Press, then half fill the bag with dried lavender.

6 Tie a ribbon bow around the bag 3½in (9cm) from the base, keeping the lavender in. Neatly work a few stitches through the knot of the bow to keep it in place. Trim the ends of the ribbon into an inverted V-shape to prevent fraying.

3 With right sides together, matching the side edges, fold the fabric in half widthways to measure 3½in (9cm) wide and then pin. Machine stitch the raw side edge.

4 Some seams will be better placed at the centre back of the work to show off the embroidered designs at the front. If so, press the seam open. Pin the lower edges and stitch. Trim the seam and cut diagonally across the corners at each end (see page 147).

Pyjamas

Made in a soft, brushed cotton, these pyjamas
will be sure to keep the chills at bay, while a silk
and cotton blend fabric will add a luxurious
touch to your nightwear.

PATTERN SHEETS

A B C
D E F

PATTERN PIECES

5	TOP FRONT
6	TOP BACK
7	FRONT FACING
8	BACK FACING
9	COLLAR
10	POCKET
11	SLEEVE
12	TROUSER BACK
	(JOIN 12A + 12B)
13	TROUSER FRONT
	(JOIN 13A + 13B)
14	PLACKET

FABRIC REQUIRED

To calculate the length of fabric you need, refer to the appropriate column for your dress size and the fabric width you are using.

FABRIC WIDTH	SMALL	MEDIUM	LARGE
36in (90cm) without nap	4⅝yd (4.2m)	4¾yd (4.4m)	4⅞yd (4.5m)
45in (115cm) without nap	4⅝yd (4.2m)	4¾yd (4.4m)	4⅞yd (4.5m)
60in (150cm) without nap	3½yd (3.2m)	3⅝yd (3.3m)	3¾yd (3.4m)
36in (90cm) iron-on interfacing	¾yd (70cm)	⅞yd (80cm)	⅞yd (80cm)

SUGGESTED FABRICS Cotton, silk and cotton blends, silk crepe-back satin, silk jersey, satin

SEWING NOTIONS

* Thread to match fabric
* 1⅜yd (1.25m) bias binding, ¾in (2cm) wide
* 4 buttons, ½in (12mm) in diameter

KEY

▨	wrong side of fabric
☐	right side of fabric
▩	interfacing

SEAM ALLOWANCES

Take ⅝in (1.5cm) seam allowances throughout, unless otherwise stated

36IN (90CM) WIDE & 45IN (115CM) WIDE

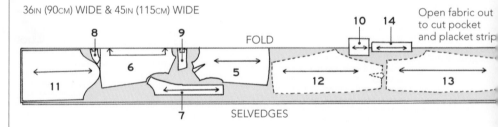

60IN (150CM) WIDE

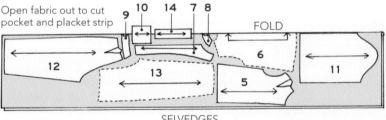

BROKEN LINES INDICATE REVERSE SIDE OF PATTERNS

PYJAMA TOP

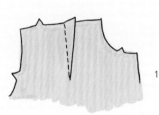

1

Stitch the shoulder darts (see page 154) on the pyjama top fronts. Press the darts (see page 157) towards the centre fronts.

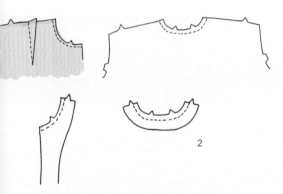

2

Staystitch (see page 152) the neck edges of the front and back tops and the front and back facings to prevent the fabric from stretching.

3

With right sides together, matching notches, pin and stitch the top front pieces to the top back piece at the shoulder seams.

Collar and facings

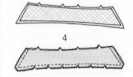

4

5

4 Following the manufacturer's instructions, apply iron-on interfacing (see page 137) to the wrong side of one collar piece. This will be the under collar. With right sides together, pin the second collar piece to the under collar. Stitch around the three outer edges. Trim the seams, snip the curves and cut diagonally across the corners (see page 147). Turn right side out and press.

5 With the right side of the under collar to the right side of the garment, matching notches at the front and back neck, pin the neck edges together. Tack the collar in place, stitching through all layers.

6 Apply iron-on interfacing to the wrong side of the left and right front facings. Stitch the front facings to the back facing at the shoulder edges. Press the seams open.

7 Turn under and press a ¼in (6mm) hem around the outside edge of the left and right front facings and the back facing. Stitch close to the pressed-under edges.

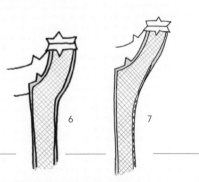

6

7

Collar and facings

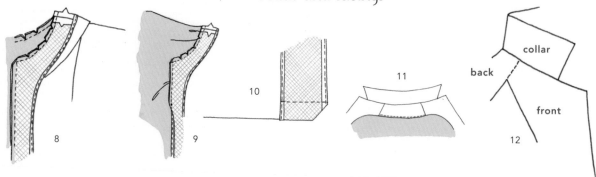

8 With right sides together, matching notches, pin the facings to the garment. Stitch along the front edges and around the neck. Trim the seam and snip the curves.

9 Press the seam at the front edges towards the facings. Sew the seam down to the facing, from the dot to the hem, working close to the previous line of stitches.

10 With right sides together, stitch across the lower edge of the front facings, allowing a 1in (2.5cm) hem. Cut diagonally across the corners, taking care not to cut into the stitching.

11 Turn right side out and press. Press the back facing to the inside of the garment. Pin the lower, turned edge of the facing to the pyjama back, then tack and stitch in place in between the shoulder seams, either by hand or by machine.

12 On the right side of the garment, run a line of stitches by hand or machine along the shoulder seam line to catch the facings down.

Pocket

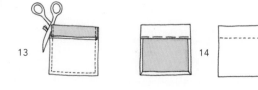

13 Press under ¼in (6mm) along the top edge of the pocket. Turn the top edge to the outside of the pocket along the fold line to form the facing. Stitch along the seam line along the side and bottom edges. Trim the seams to ¼in (6mm).

14 Turn the facing to the inside. Turn under the raw edges along the stitch line from the previous step and press. Tack the facing down, close to the turned edge. Topstitch (see page 152) along the tacking line, then remove the tacking stitches.

15 Pin the pocket to the right side of the left front, matching the dots. Tack and then stitch in place, stitching close to the side and lower edges.

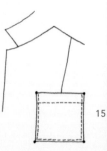

Sleeves and side seams

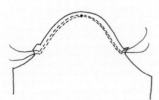

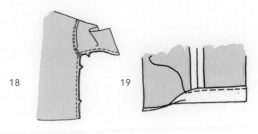

16 Run two rows of gathering stitches (see page 155) in between the notches, by hand or using a long machine stitch, working one row along the seam line and the other ¼in (6mm) inside the seam line, to ease the fullness of the top of the sleeve.

18 Stitch the sleeve and side seams, matching notches and underarm seams.

19 Turn under and press ¼in (6mm) on the lower edge of the sleeve. Turn up the hem and press. Stitch close to the turned edge.

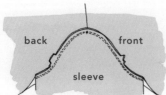

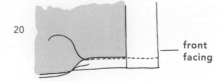

17 With right sides together, pin the sleeve to the armhole, aligning the centre dot with the shoulder seam. Match notches and seam lines at the underarms. Pull up the gathering stitches to fit. Tack the sleeve in place, easing in the fullness. Stitch the underarm seams, then work a second line of stitches close to the first for added strength. Trim each side of the seam allowance separately, from the underarm to the notch. Press the seam towards the sleeve.

20 Turn under and press ¼in (6mm) on the hem, tucking it under behind the front facings. Turn up the hem and press. Stitch close to the pressed edge, working right across the front facings to the end.

Finishing off

21 Work three buttonholes (see pages 160–1) on the right front, as indicated on the pattern. Lap the right front over the left, matching the centre front. Mark the position of buttons to correspond with the buttonholes. Attach the buttons.

PYJAMA TROUSERS

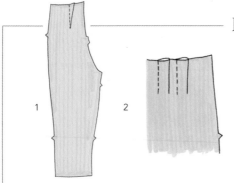

Darts and pleats

1 Stitch the darts (see page 154) in the trouser back pieces and press towards the centre backs.

2 To make the pleats in the trouser fronts, fold the fabric along the solid lines. Tack along the broken lines. Stitch down the tacking line from the waist for 1½in (4cm). Press the pleats towards the trouser side seam.

Side opening

3 With right sides together, matching notches, stitch the right front and back leg pieces together along the side seam. Repeat with the left front and back leg pieces, leaving an opening from the waist to the first notch on the left trouser leg for the fastening. Press the seam open.

4 With the right side of the placket strip to the wrong side of the left trouser leg opening, pin and stitch the placket strip down one side of the opening and up the other. Trim the seam and press towards the placket strip.

5 Turn under and press ⅝in (1.5cm) on the other side of the placket strip.

6 Fold the strip so that the pressed edge meets the line of stitching on the right side of the trouser leg. Pin and slipstitch by hand (see page 151) or machine stitch in place.

7 Turn in the piece on the front edge to form the facing and tack in place at the waist. Leave the back edge of the placket at the outside of the garment. Stitch a diagonal line at the fold to prevent it from turning to the outside.

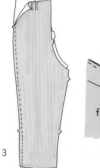
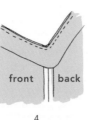

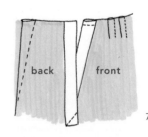

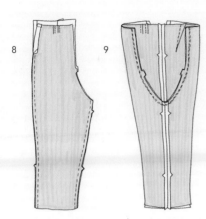

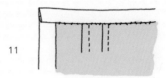

11 Trim the seam and press the bias binding to the inside. Slipstitch the bias binding in place on the inside of the waist.

8 With right sides together, matching the notches, stitch the inside leg seams.

9 With right sides together, matching the notches at the front and back, slip one leg inside the other. Pin and stitch from the front waist, across the leg seams and up to the back waist. It is a good idea to work a second row of stitches over the first on this seam for added strength. Turn the trousers right side out.

12 Turn under 1in (2.5cm) at the hem and press. Turn the raw edge under and press, then stitch the hem.

13 Work a buttonhole (see pages 160–1) at the opening of the front waist, as indicated on the pattern. Sew a button to the back waist to correspond with the buttonhole.

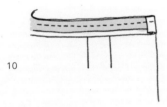

10 Open out one edge of the bias binding and, with right sides together, pin and stitch the creased line of the binding to the waist, turning under the raw edges at the side opening.

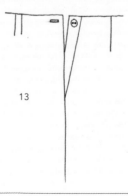

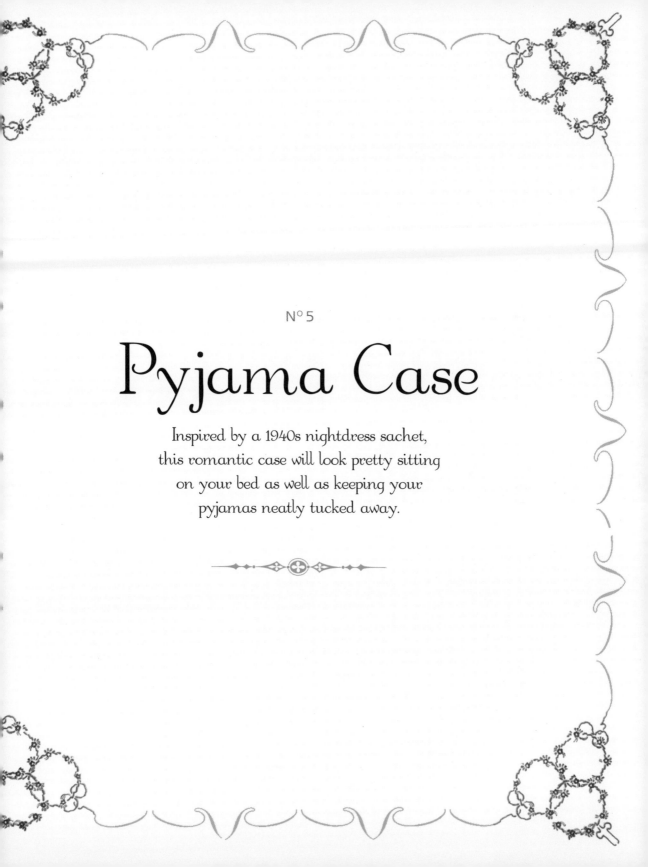

Pyjama Case

Inspired by a 1940s nightdress sachet,
this romantic case will look pretty sitting
on your bed as well as keeping your
pyjamas neatly tucked away.

FABRIC REQUIRED

To calculate the length of fabric you need, refer to the appropriate row for the fabric width you are using.

MAIN FABRIC AND LINING FABRIC WIDTH

36in (90cm) without nap	1yd (90cm) of each
45in (115cm) without nap	1yd (90cm) of each
60in (150cm) without nap	⅞yd (80cm) of each

WADDING WIDTH

27in (69cm)	1yd (90cm)
54in (137cm)	½yd (45cm)

SUGGESTED FABRICS Pyjama case: Taffeta, satin, cotton sateen.
Flower: A selection of mixed fabric oddments such as cotton, cotton sateen, chiffon, silk, georgette, voile, taffeta.

SEWING NOTIONS

* Thread to match fabric
* Millinery stiffener
* 105 x 4mm beads
* Fine nylon bead thread
* Beading needle or fine sewing needle

SEAM ALLOWANCES

Take ⅝in (1.5cm) seam allowances throughout, unless otherwise stated

FINISHED SIZES

Pyjama case: Approx. 15½ x 16½in (39 x 42cm)
Flower: 7in (18cm) in diameter

KEY

wrong side of fabric
right side of fabric

36IN (90CM) & 45IN (115CM)

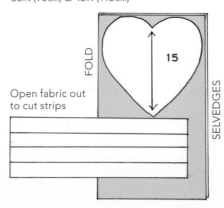

FOLD

Open fabric out
to cut strips

15

SELVEDGES

60IN (150CM)

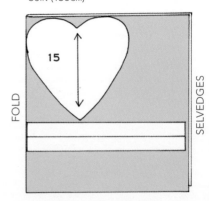

FOLD

15

SELVEDGES

PYJAMA CASE

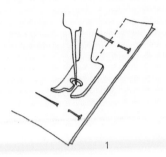

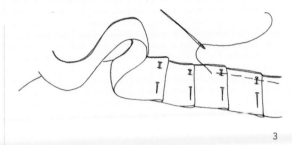

1

3

Cut two pattern 15 pieces each from main fabric, lining fabric and wadding. Cut four 29½ x 3in (75 x 7.5cm) strips from the main fabric. With right sides together, pin and stitch the short edges of the strips together to form one long ring.

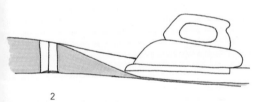

2

Press the seams of the ring open (see page 157). With wrong sides together, fold the ring in half lengthways and press.

3 Match a seam on the long ring of folded fabric to the pointed end at the base of the heart on the right side of the one main fabric piece and pin in place, aligning the raw edges of the ring with the raw edge of the main fabric. Pin the seam that is half way around the ring in between the top shaping. Fold each half of the ring of fabric into evenly spaced pleats to fit around half the edge of the heart. Pin the pleats down as you go and then tack in place, taking care to ease them around the pointed end. Alternatively, gather the frill by working a running stitch by hand or long machine stitch and pulling the threads up to fit each side of the heart.

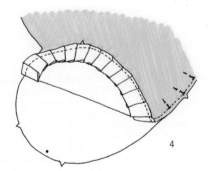

4

4 With right sides together, matching notches and with the pleated edging facing in towards the centre of the heart, pin the front and back main fabric pieces together.

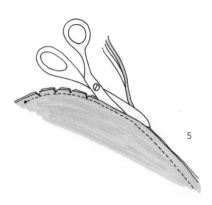

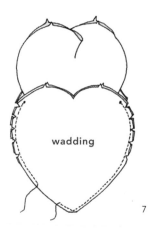

5   Stitch the lower edges between the dots. Trim the seam and notch the curves and cut across the angle at the pointed tip (see page 147). Turn right side out and press.

7   Slip the main fabric heart inside the padded lining, with right side of main fabric to the lining and the wadding facing out. Pin in place through all layers, matching the seam joining the front and back, and the notches around the top shaping between the dots.

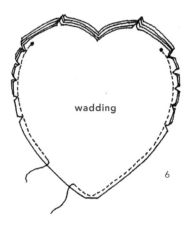

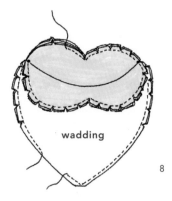

6   With right sides together, place the two lining pieces between the two pieces of wadding. Stitch the lower edges between the dots, leaving an opening near the pointed tip of around 4in (10cm). Trim the seam, notch the curves and cut the angle at the pointed tip.

8   Stitch around the top, shaped edge, between the dots. Trim the seam, notch the curves and snip in between the top shaping, near the stitch line, so that the seam lays flat. Turn right side out and slipstitch (see page 151) the opening to close the seam. Push the padded lining into the inside of the pyjama case. Work a few stitches through all thicknesses at the pointed base to hold the padded lining in place.

FLOWER

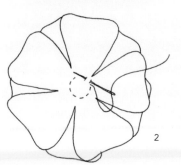

1   2   3

Enlarge the pyjama case flower templates on page 170 by 400% and cut out. Cut two small, two medium and two large flowers from the fabric. Following the manufacturer's instructions, coat the petals with millinery stiffener and allow to dry completely before commencing.

Starting with the smallest petals, place one set over the other so that the top layer of petals lies in between those of the set below. Run a gathering stitch (see page 155) around the centre of the petals, as indicated by the broken line on the pattern pieces. Draw up the thread and fasten off.

Gather the medium petals as for the small set. As you do so, slip the excess fabric at the centre of the underside of the small petals into the gathered centre of the medium petals. Draw up the gathering thread of the medium petals to close tightly around the excess fabric of the small petals and stitch the layers together. Repeat for the largest set of petals.

4   For the stamen, cut a length of nylon beading thread and, using a needle, fasten the end to the back of the flower and thread through to the front. Next, remove the needle and thread 15 beads onto the nylon. Miss the last bead and thread the nylon back through the remaining 14 beads. Make sure that the first bead sits against the flower before using a needle to thread the beaded nylon through to the back of the work.

5   Bring the thread through to the front of the flower and repeat the process until you have seven stamens. Attach the finished flower to the front of the pyjama case.

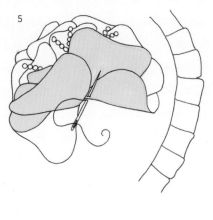

5

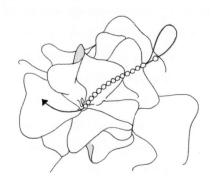

4

Bra Top

The adjustable straps make this bra top very versatile. They can be tied in a bow as a halter neck, buttoned with the straps crossed at the back, or simply worn straight over the shoulders.

PATTERN PIECES

16 FRONT
17 BACK
18 STRAP

FABRIC REQUIRED

To calculate the length of fabric you need, refer to the appropriate column for your dress size and the fabric width you are using.

FABRIC WIDTH	SMALL	MEDIUM	LARGE
36in (90cm) without nap	½yd (45cm) main	½yd (45cm) main	½yd (45cm) main
	½yd (45cm) lining	½yd (45cm) lining	½yd (45cm) lining
45in (115cm) without nap	⅜yd (40cm) main	½yd (45cm) main	½yd (45cm) main
	⅜yd (40cm) lining	½yd (45cm) lining	½yd (45cm) lining
60in (150cm) without nap	⅓yd (30cm) main	⅜yd (40cm) main	⅜yd (40cm) main
	⅓yd (30cm) lining	⅜yd (40cm) lining	⅜yd (40cm) lining

SUGGESTED FABRICS Silk crepe-back satin, silk habotai, cotton, cotton blends, crepe

SEWING NOTIONS

* Thread to match fabric
* 4in (10cm) elastic, ⅛in (3mm) wide
* 6 buttons, ⅜in (1cm) in diameter

KEY

◻ wrong side of fabric
◻ right side of fabric

SEAM ALLOWANCES

Take ⅝in (1.5cm) seam allowances throughout, unless otherwise stated

36IN (90CM) WIDE

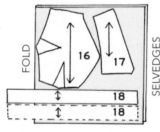

45IN (115CM) WIDE

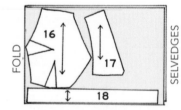

OPEN OUT FABRIC TO CUT STRAPS

60IN (150CM) WIDE

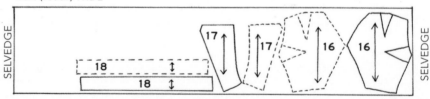

BROKEN LINES INDICATE REVERSE SIDE OF PATTERNS

Darts and side seams

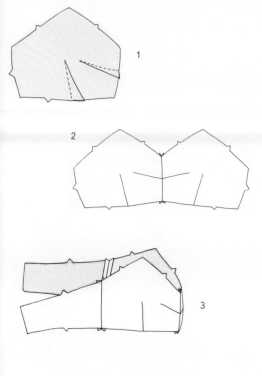

1

2

3

1 Stitch the darts (see page 154) on the fronts of the outer and lining pieces. Press the bust darts (see page 157) towards the centre front and the centre front dart down.

2 With right sides together, matching notches and dart seams, pin and stitch the front outer pieces together at the centre front. Repeat with the front lining pieces. Trim the seams and press open.

3 With right sides together and matching notches, stitch the front and back side seams of the outer pieces. Repeat with the front and back lining pieces. Trim the seams and press open.

Lining

4 With right sides together, pin and stitch the outer to the lining, leaving an opening at the right back edge to turn. Trim the seams, notch the curves and cut diagonally across the corners, taking care not to cut into the stitching (see page 147).

5 Turn right side out and press, turning under the raw edges at the opening. Cut the elastic in two equal lengths. Fold each piece in half and slip inside the opening at the small dots on the centre back. Pin and tack in place.

6 Topstitch (see page 152) all around the outside edge. Run a second line of stitches ⅛in (3mm) from the first on the back edges only.

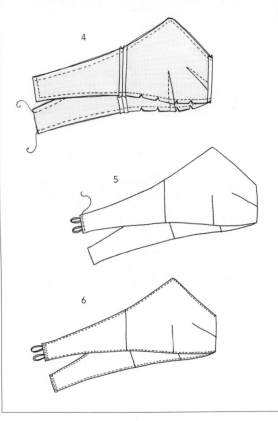

4

5

6

Straps

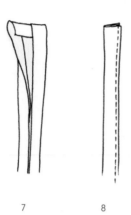

7   8

7 On each strap piece, turn under ¼in (6mm) at both short edges, turn the long edges in to meet in the centre and press.

8 Fold the strap in half lengthways and topstitch near the edge.

9 Pin and stitch the straps to the inside front of the bra top at the dots on the pattern piece.

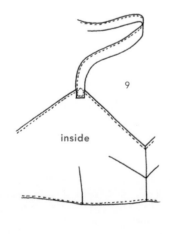

9

inside

Finishing touches

10 Work a buttonhole (see pages 160–1) on each side of the back, as indicated on the pattern piece.

11 Sew buttons in place at the back to correspond with the elastic loops, adjusting the position to fit, if necessary.

12 Mark the position for two buttons at the end of each strap – one where each strap lies straight over the shoulder from the front to the back, and the other to fasten when crossing the straps over at the back, adjusting the position to fit comfortably. Attach the remaining buttons at these points.

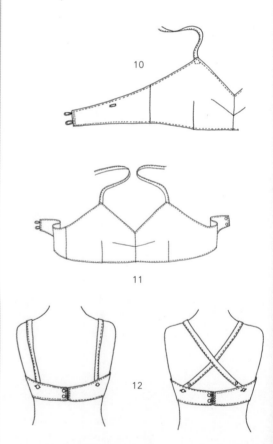

10

11

12

'Brevity is the soul of lingerie.'

DOROTHY PARKER

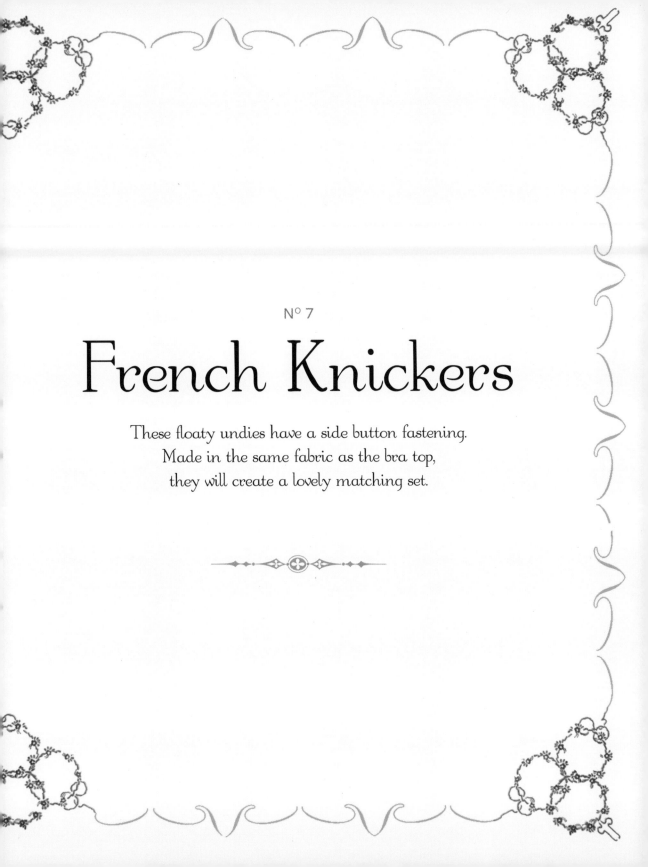

French Knickers

These floaty undies have a side button fastening.
Made in the same fabric as the bra top,
they will create a lovely matching set.

PATTERN SHEET

B

PATTERN PIECES

19 FRONT
20 BACK
21 PLACKET
22 GUSSET

FABRIC REQUIRED

To calculate the length of fabric you need, refer to the appropriate column for your dress size and the fabric width you are using.

FABRIC WIDTH	SMALL	MEDIUM	LARGE
36in (90cm) without nap	1¼yd (1.1m)	1⅓yd (1.2m)	1⅓yd (1.2m)
45in (115cm) without nap	1¼yd (1.1m)	1⅓yd (1.2m)	1⅓yd (1.2m)
60in (150cm) without nap	¾yd (70cm)	1⅓yd (1.2m)	1⅓yd (1.2m)

SUGGESTED FABRICS Silk crepe-back satin, silk habotai, cotton, cotton blends, crepe

SEWING NOTIONS

* Thread to match fabric
* Small remnant of cotton fabric for gusset, approx. 10 x 10in (26 x 26cm)
* 3⅝yd (3.3m) bias binding, ½in (12mm) wide
* 3 buttons, ⅜in (1cm) in diameter

SEAM ALLOWANCES

Take ⅝in (1.5cm) seam allowances throughou unless otherwise stated

KEY

wrong side of fabric
right side of fabric

36IN (90CM) & 45IN (115CM) ALL SIZES
60IN (150CM) MEDIUM & LARGE SIZES

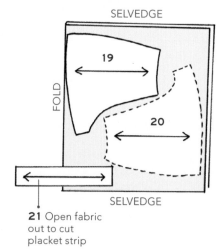

21 Open fabric out to cut placket strip

60IN (150CM) WIDE – SMALL SIZE ONLY

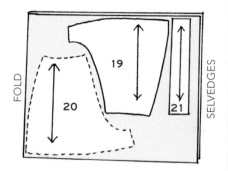

COTTON REMNANT

BROKEN LINES INDICATE REVERSE SIDE OF PATTERNS

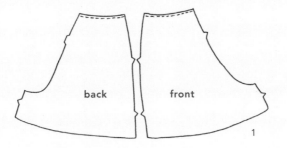

1. Staystitch (see page 152) around the waist of the front and back pieces to prevent the fabric from stretching.

With right sides together, stitch the centre front seam. Snip the curves (see page 147) and press the seam open (see page 157).

With right sides together, stitch the centre back seam. Snip the curves and press the seam open.

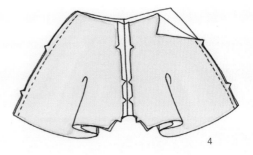

4. With right sides together, stitch the side seams, leaving an opening from the waist to the first notch on the left side for the fastening.

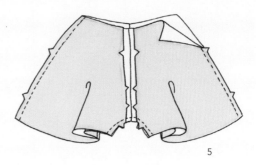

5. With right sides together, stitch the inside leg seam. Press the seam open.

Side fastening

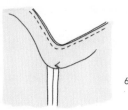

6

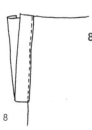

8

8 Fold the strip so that the pressed edge meets the line of stitching on the right side of the knickers. Pin and slipstitch by hand (see page 151) or machine stitch in place.

6 With the right side of the placket strip to the wrong side of the fabric, pin and stitch the strip down one side of the opening and up the other. Trim the seam and press towards the placket strip.

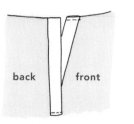

back   front   9

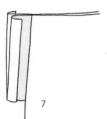

7

7 Turn under and press ⅝in (1.5cm) on the other side of the placket strip.

9 Turn in the piece on the front edge to form the facing and tack in place at waist. Leave the back edge of the placket strip at the outside of the garment. Tack along the fold of the placket to hold it in position at the front of the knickers. Sew in place, then remove the tacking stitches.

Binding the waistline

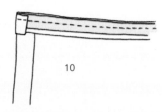

10

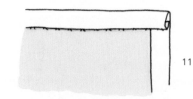

11

10 Open out one edge of the bias binding and, with right sides together, pin and stitch the creased line of the binding to the waist at the seam line, turning under the raw edges at the side opening.

11 Trim the seam and clip the curves. Press the bias binding to the inside and stitch in place around the waist by hand or machine.

Gusset

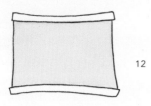

12

12 Turn under ⅝in (1.5cm) at the top and bottom edges of the gusset and press.

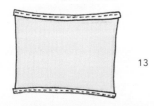

13

13 Stitch ⅛in (3mm) from the edge. Trim the seam close to the stitching.

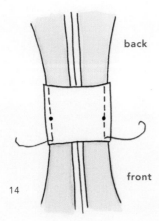

back

front

14

14 Pin the gusset to the inside of the knickers at the crotch, matching the inside leg seam to the dots. Smooth the fabric across the inside leg seam and tack in place at the hem on each side, leaving the turned edges free.

Hem

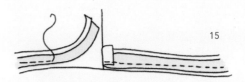

15

15 Open out one edge of the bias binding and turn under the end. With right sides together, pin and stitch the creased line of the binding to the hem of the leg at the seam line, starting at the inside leg seam. Overlap the binding at the end to neaten.

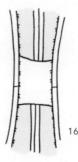

16

16 Trim the seam of the hem and gusset. Press the bias binding to the inside. Stitch in place around the leg by hand or machine. Bind the hem of the other leg in the same way.

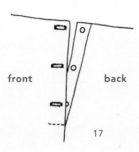

front   back

17

17 Work three buttonholes (see pages 160–1) at the front edge of the side opening of the knickers, as indicated on the pattern. Sew the buttons to the back edge of the side opening, to correspond with the buttonholes.

Hosiery Sachet

Keep your delicate silks or nylons tidy
in a pretty satin sachet. A window cut into
the centre of the embroidered flower pot makes
it easy to identify the shade of the contents.

FABRIC REQUIRED
6¾ x 19in (17 x 48.25cm) main fabric

SUGGESTED FABRICS Silk satin, silk crepe-back satin, polyester satin

SEWING NOTIONS
* Thread to match fabric
* Stranded embroidery threads in pink, green, gold and black
* 14in (35.5cm) ribbon, ¼in (6mm) wide
* Dressmaker's carbon paper

SEAM ALLOWANCES
Take ⅝in (1.5cm) seam allowances throughout, unless otherwise stated

FINISHED SIZE
7⅝ x 5¼in (19.5 x 13.5cm)

KEY
░ wrong side of fabric
☐ right side of fabric

Embroidery

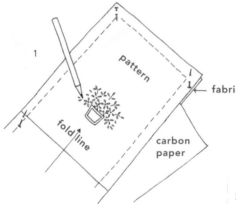

1 Cut the fabric to size. Enlarge the template on page 170 by 320% and place on top of the fabric. Transfer the embroidery motif to the fabric by slipping dressmaker's carbon paper, carbon side down, between the template and the right side of the fabric, and tracing over the design with a pencil.

2 Using three strands of embroidery thread, work French knots for the flower centres in gold, lazy daisy stitch in pink for the petals and green for the leaves, and stem stitch in green for the stems. Work the flower pot in buttonhole stitch with black thread. (See pages 164–5 for stitches.) Use a pressing cloth and press with a warm iron on the reverse to avoid flattening the embroidery too much.

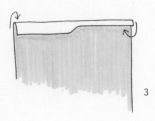

Turn under a ⅝in (1.5cm) hem at the short ends of the fabric and press. Turn the raw edge under once again, press and stitch.

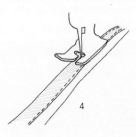

Cut a length of ribbon to fit across the lower end of the work and stitch it in place just a little way up from the edge. Press with a warm iron.

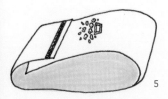

With wrong sides of the fabric together, fold the work into a bag shape, as indicated on the pattern, so that the short folded end forms a flap over the embroidered front of the sachet. Press and pin the side edges, pinning through all three layers of fabric at the top end.

6   Stitch the sides using a French seam, as follows: with the wrong sides of the work to the inside, stitch the side seams ¼in (6mm) from the edge. Press the seams flat and trim close to the stitching.

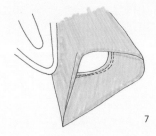

7   Turn the work wrong side out. The flap will be tucked in the inside of the bag. Carefully push the corners out with a pencil and press the side seams.

8   Pin and sew along the seams, taking a ⅜in (1cm) seam. This will enclose the raw edge and finishes the French seam.

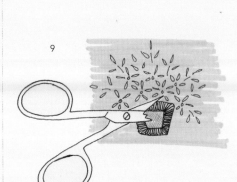

9   Carefully cut out the centre of the flower pot, close to the stitching, with a small pair of sharp-pointed scissors. Press the seams, then turn the sachet right side out and press again.

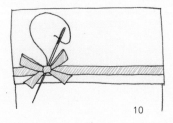

10 Tie the remaining ribbon in a bow and sew to the ribbon stitched across the sachet flap.

Slip

This lace-trimmed slip with gathered bodice
is designed to fit comfortably under a frock.
Glamorous in silk crepe, it would be just as
pretty in a dainty floral cotton lawn.

CD

PATTERN PIECES

23 BODICE
24 BACK
25 FRONT

FABRIC REQUIRED

To calculate the length of fabric you need, refer to the appropriate column for your dress size and the fabric width you are using.

FABRIC WIDTH	SMALL	MEDIUM	LARGE
36in (90cm) without nap	1⅞yd (1.7m)	1⅞yd (1.7m)	2yd (1.8m)
45in (115cm) without nap	1⅞yd (1.7m)	1⅞yd (1.7m)	2yd (1.8m)
60in (150cm) without nap	1yd (90cm)	1⅛yd (1m)	1⅛yd (1m)

SUGGESTED FABRICS Crepe, silk crepe-de-chine, silk crepe-back satin, satin, voile, cotton poplin, lawn

SEWING NOTIONS

* Thread to match fabric
* 1⅓yd (1.2m) bias binding, ½in (12mm) wide
* 39in (1m) ribbon, ⅜in (1cm) wide
* 3⅛yd (2.9m) lace, ¾–2in (2–5cm) wide

FINISHED MEASUREMENTS

Back length from shoulder
Small: 38in (96.5cm)
Medium: 39¼in (100cm)
Large: 39⅜in (103.5cm)

Width around hem
Small: 54in (137cm)
Medium: 57½in (146cm)
Large: 61½in (156cm)

SEAM ALLOWANCES

Take ⅝in (1.5cm) seam allowances throughout unless otherwise stated

KEY

◾ wrong side of fabric
☐ right side of fabric

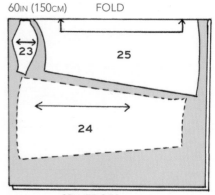

60IN (150CM)   FOLD

SELVEDGES

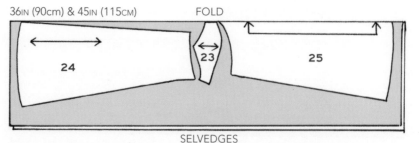

36IN (90CM) & 45IN (115CM)   FOLD

SELVEDGES

BROKEN LINES INDICATE REVERSE SIDE OF PATTERNS

1 Staystitch (see page 152) ¼in (6mm) from the top raw edges of the bodice and back pieces to prevent the fabric from stretching.

2 With right sides together, matching notches, stitch the centre back seam. Press the seam open (see page 157).

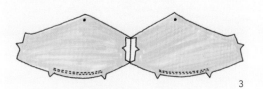

3

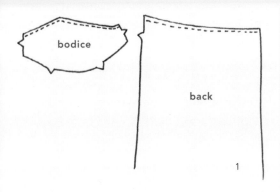

bodice

back

1

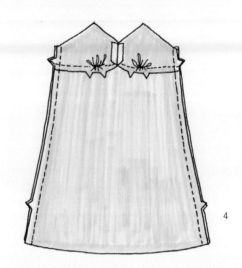

4

front

2

3 Run two rows of gathering stitches (see page 155) in between the notches on the front bodice pieces, by hand or using a long machine stitch, working one row along the seam line and the other ¼in (6mm) inside the seam line. With right sides together, matching notches, stitch the bodice pieces together at the centre front. Press the seam open.

4 With right sides together, matching notches and matching the centre seam to the shaped centre front, pin the bodice to the front. Adjust the gathers to fit. Tack and stitch. With right sides together, matching notches, stitch the front to the back at the side seams. Press the seams open.

Binding

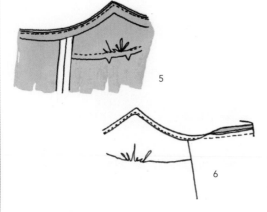

5

6

5 Open out one edge of the bias binding and, with the right side of the binding to the wrong side of the garment, pin the creased line of the binding close to the top edge of the back and the bodice front. Stitch in place along the crease.

6 Trim the seam and press the bias binding to the outside of the garment. Tack and topstitch (see page 152) the bias binding in place.

Hem

7 Turn under ⅝in (1.5cm) at the hem and press. To ease in the fullness of the skirt, stitch ¼in (6mm) from raw edge, using a long machine stitch. Pull up the machine stitching so that the hem lies flat. Now turn under the edge along the stitching and press. Stitch in place.

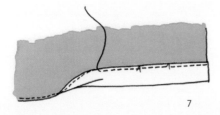

7

Lace trim

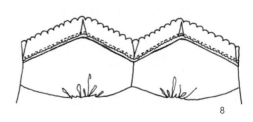

8

8 Pin the lace close to the top edge of the bias binding on the right side of the garment, starting at the side seam and working right across the back. Turn the lace under at the ends to neaten. Take time to neatly fold the fullness at the side seams, centre front and bodice shaping. Stitch the lace in place by hand or using a straight or zig-zag stitch on the machine (see page 148), then stitch the folds by hand or using a zig-zag machine stitch.

9 On the outside of the hem, pin the lace around the lower edge, turning under the ends at the seam to neaten. Stitch in place.

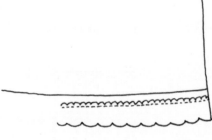

9

'Look your best –
who said love is blind?'

MAE WEST

— Straps —

10 Cut the ribbon into two equal lengths. On the inside of the slip, sew one length of ribbon to each side of the centre back at the dots, stitching the ribbon over the bound edge and all the way up to the top of the lace trim, turning under the ends to neaten.

11 Pin the other ends of the ribbon to the inside of the front of the bodice at the dots. Adjust to fit and sew to the bound edge, turning under the ends to neaten and catching the ribbon with neat stitches where it meets the lace trim.

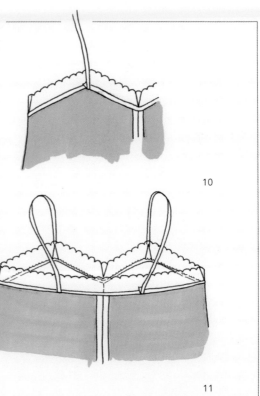

10

11

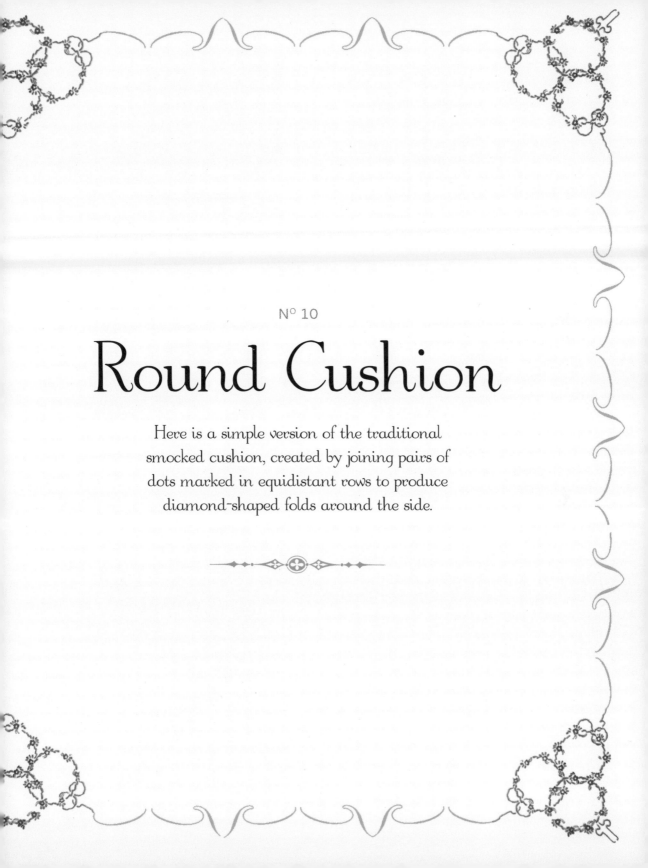

Round Cushion

Here is a simple version of the traditional
smocked cushion, created by joining pairs of
dots marked in equidistant rows to produce
diamond-shaped folds around the side.

FABRIC REQUIRED

To calculate the length of fabric you need for the cushion pad, refer to the appropriate row for the fabric width you are using.

CUSHION COVER	2⅛ x ½yd (195 x 45cm), plus extra for buttons
CUSHION PAD FABRIC WIDTH	
36in (90cm) without nap	27in (70cm)
45in (115cm) without nap	24in (60cm)
60in (150cm) without nap	24in (60cm)

SUGGESTED FABRICS Silk shantung, silk dupion, satin, linen and silk mix, wool crepe; polyester cotton blend for the cushion pad

SEWING NOTIONS

* Thread to match fabric
* Stranded embroidery thread in matching or contrasting shade
* Embroidery needle
* Toy stuffing
* 1½in (38mm) self-cover buttons x 2
* 2in (5cm) elastic, ¼in (6mm) wide
* Long, large-eyed, sharp needle (for the elastic)

FINISHED SIZE

12in (30cm) in diameter

SEAM ALLOWANCES

Take ⅝in (1.5cm) seam allowances throughout, unless otherwise stated

KEY

wrong side of fabric
right side of fabric

Cushion pad

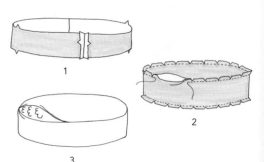

1 With right sides together, matching notches, pin and stitch the short edges of the pad side pieces together to form a ring. Press the seams open (see page 157).

2 With right sides together, matching the notches and dots, pin and stitch the top and base to the side piece, leaving an opening of about 6in (15cm) in the top. Trim and notch the seam (see page 147).

3 Turn the cushion pad right side out, fill with stuffing and slipstitch (see page 151) the opening closed.

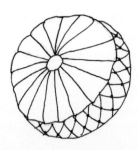

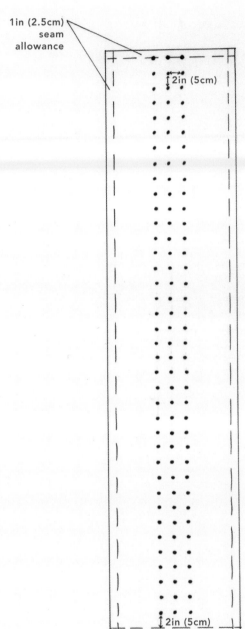

1in (2.5cm) seam allowance

2in (5cm)

2in (5cm)

4

4 Mark the centre of the cushion-cover fabric with pins or long stitches. On the right side of the fabric, mark out 38 dots at 2in (5cm) intervals along the length of the central line, marking the first dot on the stitch line. On each side, mark another 38 dots running parallel 2in (5cm) from the first row. There should be a 2in (5cm) gap between the last dot and the stitch line at the end of the fabric. You will have 114 dots in all.

5 With right sides together, pin and stitch the short ends of the fabric together to form a ring. Trim the seam to ½in (12mm) and press open. Turn the ring right side out.

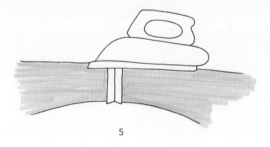

5

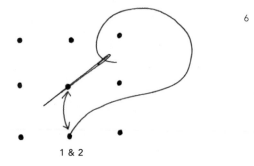

6

1 & 2

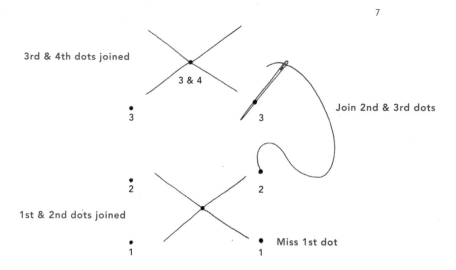

7

3rd & 4th dots joined

3 & 4

3

Join 2nd & 3rd dots

3

1st & 2nd dots joined

2

2

1

Miss 1st dot

1

6 Begin at the central line of dots, using two strands of embroidery thread. Join the first and second dots by working a small stitch through them both and drawing them together. Work a few stitches over each other and fasten off. Join the next two dots along the central line in the same way. Continue to the end of the central line of dots.

7 Begin on the line of dots to the left or right of the central line. Miss the first dot and join the next two, as before. Continue to the end of the line, then repeat on the remaining line of dots. This creates the decorative smocking effect.

Pleats

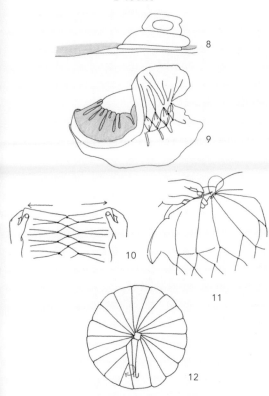

8 Turn under 1in (2.5cm) along both long edges of the ring and press.

9 Slip the cushion pad into the cover, making sure that the smocked area covers the side of the pad.

10 Pull on both edges to neaten the smocking and define the pleats formed by smocking the fabric.

11 Bring the edge of each pleat over to meet the top corner of the next pleat, lay it flat and hand stitch it in place to secure. Tuck the excess fold of the fabric under the pleats for a neat finish.

12 Tuck the fold of the last pleat under the first and stitch in place. Repeat steps 10 to 12 to finish the pleats on the other side.

Finishing touches

13 Cut a circle of fabric to size to cover the button, plus about ½in (12mm) extra all around.

14 Many self-cover buttons have teeth to hook the fabric onto; if yours do not, run a line of gathering stitches (see page 155) by hand around the edge of the fabric. Place the button dome on the wrong side of the fabric and cover the sides by hooking the material onto the teeth or gathering up the circular fabric around it, and secure with a few stitches.

15 Slip the button back over the shank, with the ridge facing down. Snap it into place. Cover another button to match the first.

16 Sew a button securely to one end of the elastic.

17 With a long needle, thread the other end of the elastic through the centre of the cushion to the other side. Stretching the elastic, sew the remaining button securely to the free end.

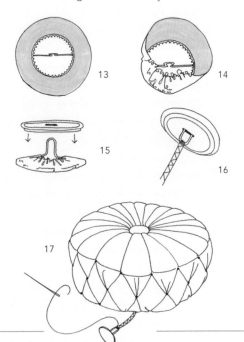

N° 11

Padded Coat Hanger

Give an old silk scarf a new lease of life
as a decorative coat hanger cover. As well
as protecting clothing, the pretty padded hanger
will show off your favourite frocks beautifully.

FABRIC REQUIRED

Main fabric large enough to fit twice the length and width of the coat hanger
Wadding to fit around hanger

SUGGESTED FABRICS Vintage silk scarf or any fabric remnant

SEWING NOTIONS

* Wooden coat hanger
* Thread to match fabric
* Length of satin ribbon
  or silk flowers to decorate

SEAM ALLOWANCES

Take ⅜in (1cm) seam allowances throughout,
unless otherwise stated

KEY

wrong side of fabric
right side of fabric

FINISHED MEASUREMENTS

Varies according to the size
of the hanger

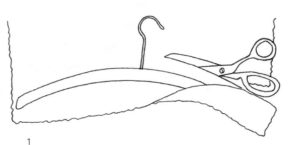

1 Cut the wadding to fit
   around the coat hanger,
   folding it over the bottom
   so that both long edges of
   the wadding meet along the
   top of the hanger.

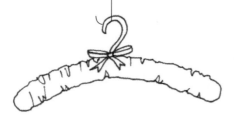

2 Cover the whole hanger, apart from the
   hook, with the wadding, pin it in place
   and stitch by hand (see page 151).

width + ¾in (2cm) each side

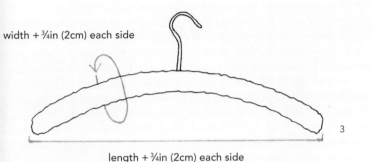

length + ¾in (2cm) each side

3

To calculate the size of fabric needed, measure around the wadded hanger and across the whole length, allowing an extra ¾in (2cm) all round. Cut two oblong pieces from the fabric using the measurements taken.

4

With right sides together, stitch the two pieces together along one short edge. Press the seam open (see page 157).

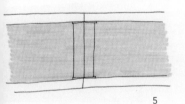

5

Turn under a hem of ⅝in (1.5cm) along both of the long edges and press.

6

6 With right sides together, fold the fabric in half lengthways. Pin and stitch the short edges together. Trim the seams and cut diagonally across the corners, taking care not to cut into the stitching. Turn right side out.

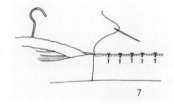

7

7 Pin together the first half of the top from the outside edge to the centre seam and join by working a neat running stitch by hand close to the edges. Without fastening off, slip the wadded coat hanger inside.

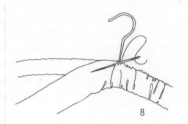

8

8 Draw up the thread, gathering the stitches along first half of the cover (see page 155) to fit snugly over the hanger with the centre seam at the hook. Work a few stitches over each other at the hook to secure in place.

9

9 Pin the remaining half of the fabric at the top edge to cover the other end of the hanger and gather as for the first side.

10 Arrange the gathers evenly across the hanger. Decorate by tying a ribbon bow or some silk flowers around the base of the hook. Secure with a few stitches.

10

Slippers

Bringing together the quilted linear sunburst
design, a lavish fabric and sparkling diamantés,
these slippers are reminiscent of the elegance
and charm of 1930s Hollywood.

FABRIC REQUIRED

½yd (45cm) main fabric, 36in (90cm) wide
8 x 16in (20 x 40.5cm) lightweight fabric for lining
½yd (45cm) wadding
16 x 16in (40 x 40cm) leather, heavyweight cotton or canvas, or denim for soles

SUGGESTED FABRICS Duchess satin, velvet, silk twill, silk dupion, taffeta

SEWING NOTIONS

* Thread to match fabric
* 2 x diamanté buckles with an interior width of ⅝–¾in (1.5–2cm)
* Cardboard (thick card from a packaging carton will be ideal)
* Dressmaker's carbon paper

SEAM ALLOWANCES

Take ⅝in (1.5cm) seam allowances throughout, unless otherwise stated

FINISHED SIZE

The pattern can be adjusted to fit any adult ladies' shoe size

KEY

wrong side of fabric
right side of fabric

Enlarging the pattern

1   Enlarge the slipper pattern pieces on page 171 so that the sole fits your foot with an extra ¾in (2cm) all around. There will be a little extra room at the front of the slipper due to the shape.

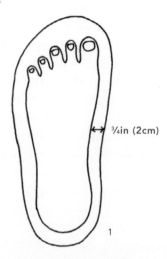

¾in (2cm)

Cutting the pieces

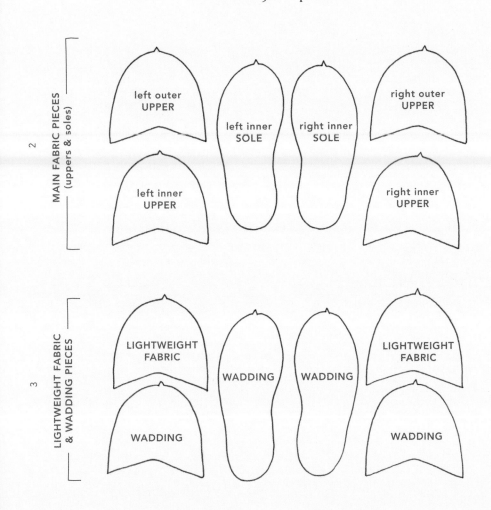

MAIN FABRIC PIECES
(uppers & soles)

2

left outer
UPPER

left inner
SOLE

right inner
SOLE

right outer
UPPER

left inner
UPPER

right inner
UPPER

**LIGHTWEIGHT FABRIC
& WADDING PIECES**

3

LIGHTWEIGHT
FABRIC

WADDING

WADDING

LIGHTWEIGHT
FABRIC

WADDING

WADDING

2 Cut four slipper uppers and one sole from the main fabric, then reverse the sole pattern and cut one sole for the other foot. This will give you one pair of outer uppers, one pair of inner uppers and one pair of inner soles.

3 Cut one upper for each foot from the lightweight fabric and one upper and one sole for each foot from the wadding.

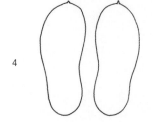

4

leather or heavyweight fabric

5

cardboard

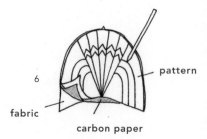

6

pattern

fabric

carbon paper

4 Cut one sole for each foot from a piece of leather, heavyweight cotton or canvas, as the fabric for the sole needs to be hard wearing; an old pair of jeans would be ideal.

5 Cut a piece of card to the shape of the sole pattern for each foot and trim away ⅝in (1.5cm) seam allowance all around. Keep the pieces for each foot in separate piles.

6 Transfer the motif to the slipper uppers by slipping carbon paper, carbon side down, between the pattern and the right side of the slipper uppers and tracing over the design with a pencil.

7 Sandwich the upper slipper wadding between the wrong side of the main fabric outer upper and the wrong side of the lightweight lining. Pin and tack the pieces together around the outside edge.

8 Work the quilted design by hand or machine on each wadded upper, following the lines on the fabric.

7

main fabric
wadding
lightweight fabric

8

Joining the uppers

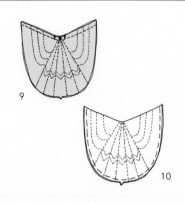

9

10

9 With right sides together, lay the quilted outer upper over the inner upper. Pin and tack around the top edge. Stitch together, taking a ⅝in (1.5cm) seam. Trim the seam and snip the curves (see page 147).

10 Turn right side out and press the seam with a warm iron (see page 157). Pin the layers of fabric and wadding together and tack around the open edges to hold them together. Now repeat steps 9 and 10 for the other upper.

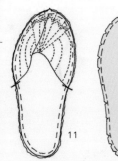
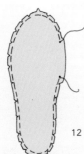

11   12

Attaching the sole

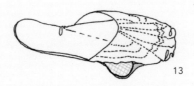

13

11 Place the upper right side up over the right side of the left inner sole, matching the notch at the toe and the corners of the upper to the lines indicated on the pattern of the sole. Place the wrong side of the left inner sole over the wadding and pin and tack in place, easing the fabric at the toe.

12 With right sides together, pin the left sole, cut from leather or heavyweight cotton fabric, over the top of the left slipper. Tack, and then stitch, taking a ⅝in (1.5cm) seam and leaving an opening between the dots. Make sure you use the correct machine needle size for the weight of the fabric you are sewing. Trim the seam and notch the curves (see page 147).

13 Turn the slipper right side out and use a knitting needle or pencil to push the fabric out at the edges. Insert the left cardboard sole into the slipper, between the wadding and the outer sole. You may need to fold back the card at the toe in order to get it in. Once the card is inside, flatten it out again and it will keep the shape of the sole.

14 Turn under the raw edges at the opening in the side of the slipper. Pin together and slipstitch (see page 151) the opening closed. Repeat steps 11–14 for the right slipper.

14

Bow

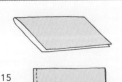

15

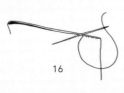

16   17

18 Sew the buckle to the slipper, folding back each side of the bow and stitching through the back and into the top of the slipper upper. Finish the other slipper in the same way.

15 With right sides together, fold the fabric for the bow in half so that the short edges meet and stitch around two sides, taking a ⅜in (1cm) seam. Trim the seam and cut diagonally across the corners (see page 147).

16 Turn the bow fabric right side out, using a knitting needle or pencil to carefully push out the corners. Press and turn under ⅜in (1cm) at the raw edge. Slipstitch to close (see page151).

17 Thread the fabric through the buckle, adjusting it so that it sits centrally and the bow is neat.

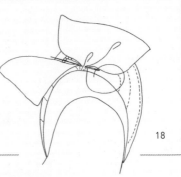

18

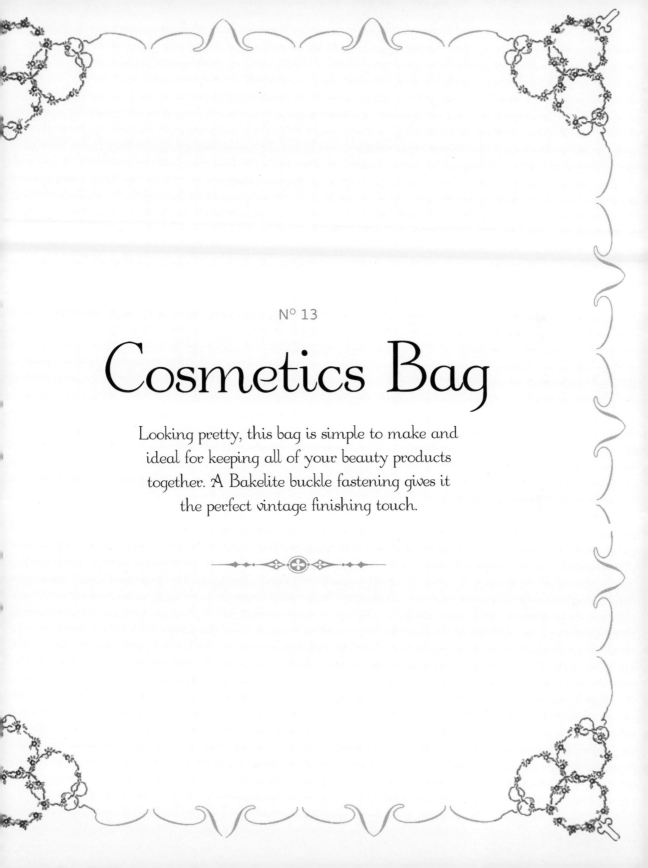

Cosmetics Bag

Looking pretty, this bag is simple to make and
ideal for keeping all of your beauty products
together. A Bakelite buckle fastening gives it
the perfect vintage finishing touch.

FABRIC REQUIRED
⅝ x ⅜yd (60 x 35cm) each of main fabric and lining

SUGGESTED FABRICS Shirting, cotton, silk habotai, silk crepe-back satin, satin, linen

SEWING NOTIONS
* Thread to match main fabric
* Stranded embroidery thread in black and silver or gold metallic
* Buckle fastening with an interior width of 1in (2.5cm)
* Dressmaker's carbon paper

SEAM ALLOWANCES
Take ⅝in (1.5cm) seam allowances throughout unless otherwise stated

FINISHED SIZE
8¼ x 6¼in (21 x 16cm)

KEY
 wrong side of fabric
right side of fabric

EMBROIDERY MOTIF (ACTUAL SIZE)

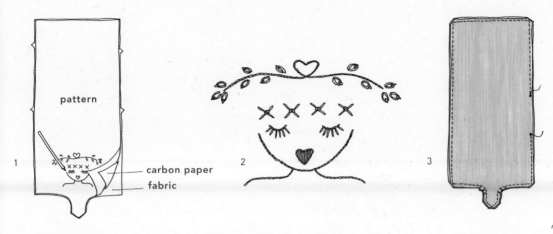

pattern

carbon paper
fabric

1

2

3

4

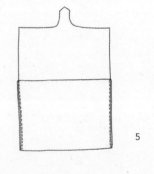

5

6

Cut one bag piece each in main fabric and lining. Trace the motif on the facing page and transfer to the main fabric by slipping dressmaker's carbon paper, carbon side down, between the motif and the right side of the fabric and tracing over the design with a pencil.

Next, using two strands of black embroidery thread, work the face, neck, shoulders, the branch above the head, the eye lines and the outline of the lips in stem stitch (see pages 164–5 for embroidery stitches). Work the eyelashes in straight stitch and fill in the heart-shaped lips in satin stitch, keeping the stitches close together. Embroider the leaves in lazy daisy stitch and four cross stitches above the eyelashes. Using two strands of silver or gold embroidery thread, work a French knot in the centre of each cross stitch. Using a pressing cloth and an iron on a warm setting, press the embroidery from the reverse (see page 157).

3   With right sides together, pin the main fabric to the lining, matching notches. Stitch around all edges, leaving an opening between the small dots, as indicated on the pattern. Trim the seams, snip the curves and cut diagonally across the corners (see page 147).

4   Turn right side out, using a knitting needle or pencil to carefully push out the corners, and press. Turn under the raw edges of the opening and slipstitch (see page 151) to close.

5   With right side out, matching the large dots, fold the short straight edge of the fabric up to form the bag. Pin and topstitch (see page 152) the sides, on the right side of the bag, close to the edges.

6   Finally, sew the buckle to the front of the bag, by working a few stitches over each other through the fabric and around the buckle bar.

Dressing Gown

With loose-fitting bell sleeves and a wide
collar, trimmed with gathered lace for a touch
of romance, this dressing gown is inspired
by a 1930s style. Enjoy repose in true
starlet fashion!

PATTERN PIECES

29 FRONT
(JOIN 29A + 29B)

30 BACK
(JOIN 30A + 30B)

31 UNDER COLLAR

32 TOP COLLAR
(JOIN 32A + 32B)

33 POCKET

34 SLEEVE
(JOIN 34A + 34B)

35 SASH
(JOIN 35A + 35B)

FABRIC REQUIRED

To calculate the length of fabric you need, refer to the appropriate column for your dress size and the fabric width you are using.

FABRIC WIDTH	SMALL	MEDIUM	LARGE
36in (90cm) without nap	8⅝yd (7.9m)	8⅞yd (8.1m)	9yd (8.2m)
45in (115cm) without nap	7¾yd (7.1m)	8yd (7.3m)	8¼yd (7.6m)
60in (150cm) without nap	6¼yd (5.7m)	6⅜yd (5.8m)	6⅝yd (6m)
36in (90cm) iron-on interfacing	1⅞yd (1.7m)	1⅞yd (1.7m)	2yd (1.8m)

SUGGESTED FABRICS Crepe, silk crepe-back satin, silk dupion, satin, wool, viscose

SEWING NOTIONS

* Thread to match fabric
* 6¼yd (5.7m) gathered lace trim
* 2⅛yd (1.9m) bias binding, ½in (12mm) wide

SEAM ALLOWANCES

Take ⅝in (1.5cm) seam allowances throughout, unless otherwise stated

FINISHED SIZE

Back length from shoulder
Small: 58in (148cm)
Medium: 60in (152cm)
Large: 61½in (156cm)

KEY

wrong side of fabric
right side of fabric
interfacing

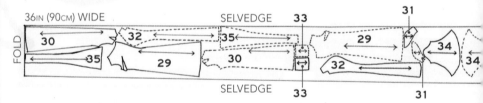

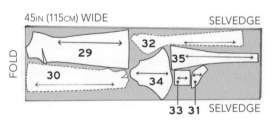

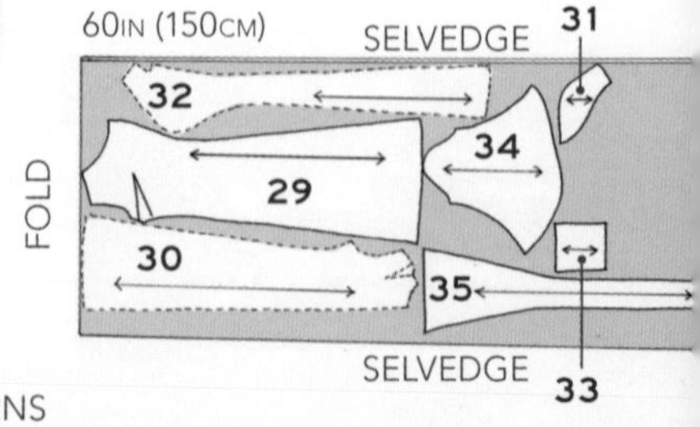

BROKEN LINES INDICATE REVERSE SIDE OF PATTERNS

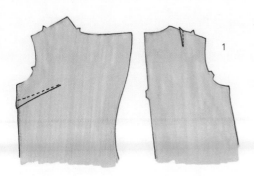

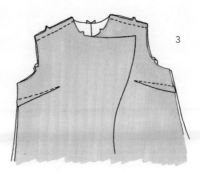

Stitch the bust darts (see page 154) on the fronts and press down (see page 157). Stitch the shoulder darts on the back and press towards the centre back.

3 With right sides together, matching notches, pin and stitch the front pieces to the back at the shoulder seams. Press the seams open.

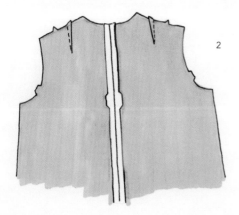

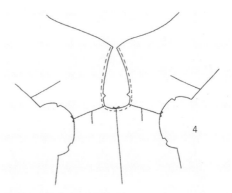

With right sides together, stitch the back pieces together at the centre back seam. Press the seam open.

4 Staystitch (see page 152) around the neck edge to prevent the fabric from stretching.

5

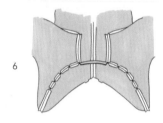

5 With right sides together, matching notches, pin and stitch the under collar pieces together at the centre back. Press the seam open.

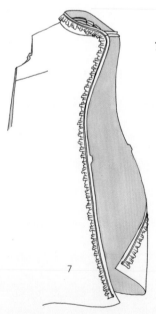

6

6 With the right side of the under collar to the right side of the dressing gown, matching notches, pin neck edges. Tack in place and stitch. Trim the seam and notch the curves. Press the seam open from the front edge to the shoulder. Press the seam in between the shoulders towards the under collar.

7 Pin the lace trim around the right side of the collar and front edges, starting and finishing at the hem line. Turn the lace under at each end to neaten. Tack in position along the seam line. Slipstitch (see page 151) the turned-under ends of the lace in place.

7

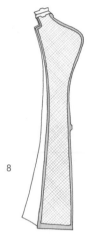

8

8 Following the manufacturer's instructions, apply iron-on interfacing (see page 137) to the wrong side of the top collar. With right sides together, matching notches, pin and stitch the top collar pieces together at the centre back. Press the seam open.

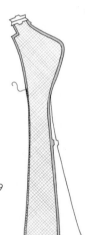

9

9 Turn under and press a ¼in (6mm) hem around the outside edge of the top collar. Stitch close to the turned edge.

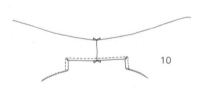

10

10 Stitch around the back neck edge to reinforce it. Clip the corners close to the stitching.

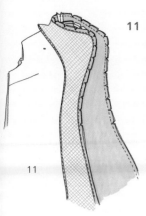

11 With right sides together, matching notches, pin the top collar to the garment and then stitch along the seam line. Trim the seam and notch the curves.

11

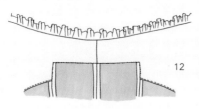

12

2 Turn the facings and collar to the inside of the garment, so that the collar is right side out, and press. Turn under the raw edge at the neckline of the collar and the shoulders, so that they meet the seam line. Slipstitch the edges down between the shoulders.

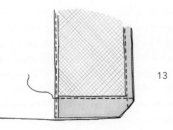

13

3 With right sides together stitch across the lower edge of the front facing, allowing a 1in (2.5cm) hem. Take care not to catch the lace in the stitches. Cut diagonally across the corners (see page 147), taking care not to cut the stitching.

Pocket

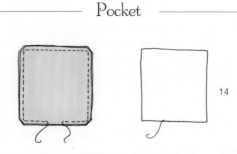

14

14 With right sides together, pin and stitch around the pocket, leaving an opening. Trim the seam and cut diagonally across the corners, taking care not to cut the stitching. Turn the pocket right side out and press. Slipstitch the opening closed.

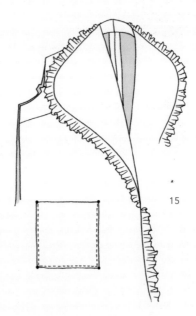

15

15 Pin the pocket to the outside of right front, matching small dots. Tack in position and stitch close to the side and lower edges.

Sleeves and side seams

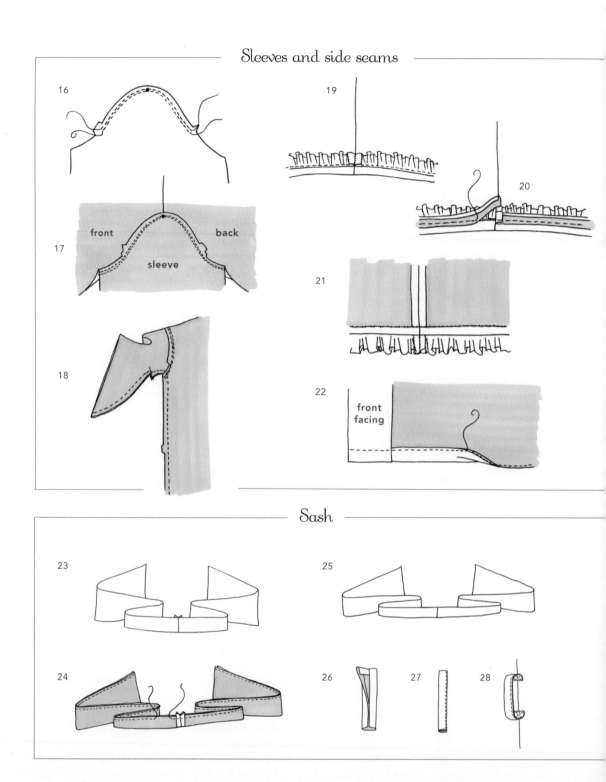

16

17 front   back

sleeve

18

19

20

21

22 front
facing

Sash

23

24

25

26   27   28

16 Run two rows of gathering stitches (see page 155) in between the notches, by hand or using a long machine stitch, working one row along the seam line and the other ¼in (6mm) inside the seam line, to ease the fullness of the top of the sleeve.

17 With right sides together, pin the sleeve to the armhole, aligning the centre dot with the shoulder seam. Match notches and seam lines at the underarms. Pull up the gathering stitches to fit. Tack the sleeve in place, easing in the fullness. Stitch the underarm seams, then work a second line of stitches close to the first for added strength. Trim each side of the seam allowance separately, from the underarm to the notch. Press the seam towards the sleeve.

18 Stitch the sleeve and side seams, matching notches and underarm seams.

19 Pin the lace trim to the hem line on the sleeve, turning under the ends at the seam to neaten. Tack and stitch in place. Slipstitch the turned-under edges of the lace trim in place.

20 Open out one edge of the bias binding and turn under the end. With right sides together, starting at the seam, pin and stitch the crease line of the binding to the seam line of the sleeve. Overlap the binding at the end to neaten.

21 Trim the seam. Press the bias binding to the inside. Stitch in place. Bind the hem of the other sleeve in the same way.

22 Turn under 1in (2.5cm) at the hem and press. To ease in the fullness, stitch ¼in (6mm) from the raw edge, using a long machine stitch. Pull up the machine stitching so that the hem lies flat. Turn under the edge along the stitching and press, tucking it under behind the front facings. Stitch in place, working right across the front facings to the end.

Sash

23 With right sides together, pin and stitch the two sash pieces together across the short end to make one long length. Press the seam open.

24 With right sides together, fold the sash along the line indicated on the pattern. Stitch all around, leaving an opening to turn. Trim the seams and cut diagonally across the corners, taking care not to cut the stitching.

25 Turn the sash right side out and press. Slipstitch the opening closed.

26 To make the loops to carry the sash, cut two 3 x 1in (8 x 2.5cm) pieces of fabric. Turn under ¼in (6mm) at each short end, turn the long edges in to the centre and press.

27 Fold the strip in half lengthways and stitch along the long, unfolded edge, close to the edge.

28 Turn under ⅜in (1cm) at each short end of each loop and stitch in place at the side seams, as indicated by the dots on the pattern. Thread the sash through the loops.

Jewellery Box

Inspiration for this design comes from old lacquered boxes inlaid with delicate mother of pearl. Embroidered silver chain stitch and pearl beads decorate the cherry blossom.

FABRIC REQUIRED

To calculate the length of fabric you need, refer to the appropriate row for the fabric width you are using.

FABRIC WIDTH

36in (90cm) without nap	12in (30cm) each of main and lining fabrics
45in (115cm) without nap	12in (30cm) each of main and lining fabrics
60in (150cm) without nap	10in (25cm) each of main and lining fabrics

WADDING WIDTH

27in (69cm)	12in (30cm)
54in (137cm)	10in (25cm)

SUGGESTED FABRICS Satin, silk shantung, silk dupion, linen

SEWING NOTIONS

* Thread to match fabric
* Stranded embroidery thread in silver
* Embroidery needle
* 8–10 small fabric cherry blossom petals
* Seed beads
* Cardboard (thick card from a packaging carton will be ideal) 11 x 11in (28 x 28cm) or enough to cut the pieces for the foundations of the box
* Tracing paper
* Tailor's chalk or dressmaker's carbon paper

SEAM ALLOWANCES

Take ⅝in (1.5cm) seam allowances throughout, unless otherwise stated

FINISHED SIZE

6 x 6 x 3in (15 x 15 x 7.5cm)

KEY

wrong side of fabric
right side of fabric

CHERRY BLOSSOM BRANCH MOTIF (ACTUAL SIZE)

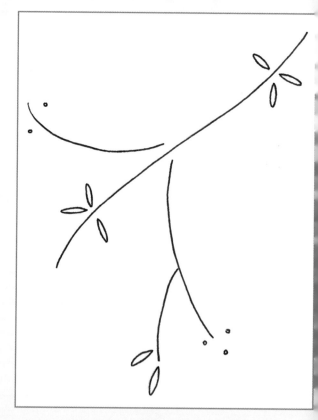

Preparing the box pieces

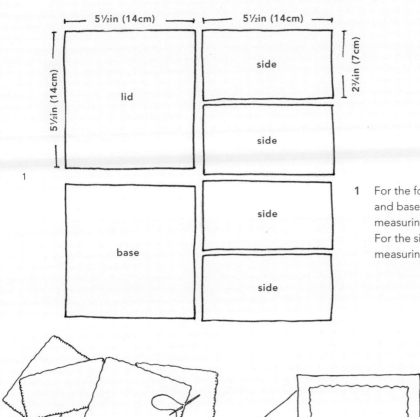

1 For the foundations of the lid and base, cut two pieces of card measuring 5½ x 5½in (14 x 14cm). For the sides, cut four pieces each measuring 5½in x 2¾in (14 x 7cm).

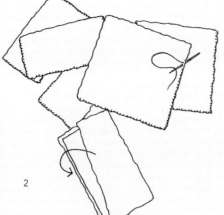

Add ⅝in (1.5cm) seam allowance all round

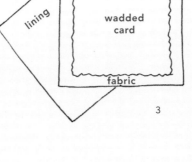

2 Cut a piece of wadding to cover both the back and front of each piece of card. Cover the card with the wadding and oversew (see page 152) by hand to keep it in place.

3 Cut a piece each from the fabric and lining to fit each wadded card plus a ⅝in (1.5cm) seam allowance all round.

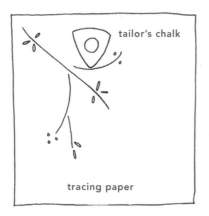

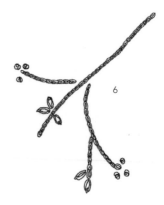

4 Trace the cherry blossom branch pattern on page 92 onto the tracing paper. Turn the tracing paper over and trace over the branch and leaves with tailor's chalk.

6 Using two strands of silver embroidery thread, work the branches in chain stitch, the leaves in lazy daisy stitches and the buds in French knots (see page 164). Press lightly with a warm iron on the reverse side (see page 157).

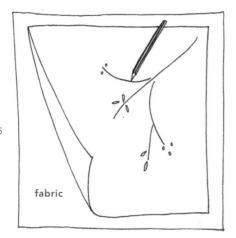

5 Lay the wrong side of the traced design over the right side of the main lid fabric and trace over the branches once again to transfer the chalk lines onto the fabric. Or, simply slip a sheet of dressmaker's carbon paper between the paper pattern and the right side of the fabric before tracing over the design.

7 Sew the silk petals in place along the blossom branches. Stitch a few seed beads to the centre of each flower to decorate.

Assembling the box

8

9

10

11   12

8   With right sides together, lay each of the main
      fabric pieces over the corresponding lining piece
      and stitch along three sides. Trim the seams and
      cut diagonally across the corners (see page 147).

9   Turn right side out and press, taking care not to
      press the cherry blossom and embroidery. Turn
      under and press a ⅝in (1.5cm) hem at the open end.

10   Slip the wadded card inside the fabric. Pin the
      pressed edges together and slipstitch (see page
      151) neatly to join.

11   To make up the box, join each side piece to
      the edges of the base, working on the outside
      in small, neat stitches. Sew up the four sides,
      stitching neatly on the outside to form the box.

12   Attach the lid to the back edge, this time by
      working on the inside of the box and joining
      both the linings. Use matching thread and
      work neatly in small stitches: this way, a little
      of the lining will show at the hinged back as
      well as around the edges.

Tassel

13   Cut a piece of card to the
      required length of your
      finished tassel. Wind the silver
      embroidery thread around the
      card to the desired thickness.
      Cut the thread, leaving a long
      length and thread through a
      needle. Slip the needle through
      all the loops on the card and

tie the thread tightly at the top
edge. Remove the card and wind
the thread around the loops, a
little way down from the tied top
end, securing with a few stitches
to fasten off. Cut through the
folded lower edge and trim to
neaten the ends. Attach the
tassel to the front of the lid.

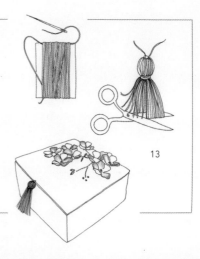

13

Hot-Water Bottle Cover

There is nothing nicer than snuggling up
with a hot-water bottle on a chilly evening.
Use a pretty vintage remnant for the cover
to make it extra cosy.

D

PATTERN PIECES

36 LOWER FRONT
37 UPPER FRONT
38 BACK

FABRIC REQUIRED

½yd (45cm) main fabric, 36in (90cm) wide
24 x 12in (60 x 30cm) piece of lightweight cotton or cotton mix for facing

SUGGESTED FABRICS Remnants of any chintz upholstery fabric

SEWING NOTIONS

* Thread to match fabric
* 45in (114.5cm) satin bias binding, ¾in (2cm) wide
* 2 buttons, 1½in (4cm) in diameter

SEAM ALLOWANCES

Take ⅝in (1.5cm) seam allowances throughout, unless otherwise stated

FINISHED SIZE

Approx. 16 x 10in (40 x 25cm)
(including bound edges)
To fit a standard 2-litre hot-water bottle

KEY

 wrong side of fabric
right side of fabric

Cutting out

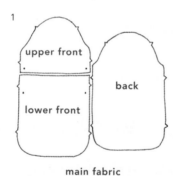

1

upper front

back

lower front

main fabric

upper front

lower front

facings

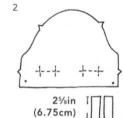

2

2⅝in (6.75cm)

1⅛in (3cm)

1 Cut an upper and lower front and a back piece from the main fabric, and an upper and lower front from facing fabric.

2 Mark the position of the buttonholes on the right side of the main fabric, as indicated on the pattern piece. Cut two strips from the main fabric measuring 2⅝in (6.75cm) long and 1⅛in (3cm) wide.

Bound buttonholes

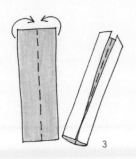

3

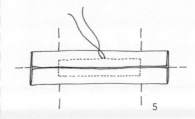

5

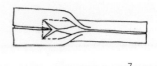

7

3 Tack (see page 151) a line of stitches down the centre of each strip of fabric. Fold both long edges over to the wrong side to meet at the centre stitching line and press (see page 157).

5 Starting in the middle of one long side, stitch ⅛in (3mm) from each side of the centre, sewing across the short ends and taking care to make them even in length. Overlap the last few stitches over the first ones.

7 Turn the strip to the inside and press.

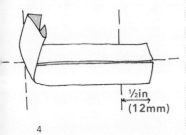

½in
(12mm)

4

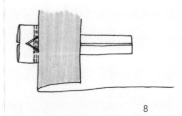

6

8

4 With the folded edges facing up, tack each strip of fabric over one set of buttonhole markings on the right side of main fabric, positioning each one centrally with ½in (12mm) extra extending beyond the markings on each side.

6 With a pair of sharp-pointed scissors, cut along the opening carefully and make a small 45-degree snip into each corner of the stitching line, taking care not to cut through the stitches.

8 With right side facing, turn back the fabric to reveal the end of the buttonhole and run a few lines of stitches across the base. Repeat for the other three ends to keep them securely in place.

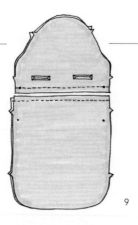

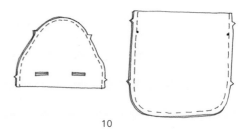

Facings

9 With right sides together, pin the facings to the main fabric pieces and stitch along the straight, top edge of the lower front piece and the lower edge of the upper front piece. Turn the pieces right side out and press.

10 Keeping the wrong sides together, pin and tack around the remaining edges.

Finishing bound buttonholes

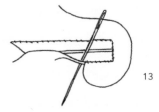

11 Pin the facing in place around the bound buttonhole. Push a pin from the right side through each corner of the buttonhole.

13 Turn under the raw edges and hem in place.

12 Cut the facing across the centre close to each end, snipping diagonally into the corners.

Joining main pieces

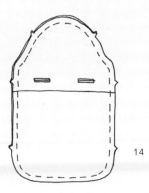

14

16

14 Place the back wrong side up on your work surface. Lay the lower front right side up on top, matching notches, then lay the upper front right side up on top, again matching notches and dots. Pin, then tack the pieces together.

16 Trim the seams to ¼in (6mm). Fold the binding to the other side of the cover, keeping the raw edge turned under. Pin and slipstitch in place (see page 151).

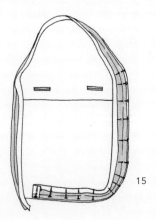

15

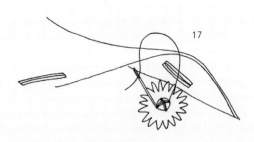

17

15 Open up one side of the bias binding. Turn under a ⅝in (1.5cm) hem at the short end of the binding and, with right sides together, pin the binding around the edge of the hot water bottle cover, overlapping the ends. Stitch in place along the crease of the binding.

17 Press the cover and the bound edges. Sew on the buttons to correspond with the buttonholes.

Sunray-Pleated Lampshade

The sunray pleats look best on an Empire
frame. Old shades can be picked up in markets
and recovered for a contemporary take
on vintage style.

FABRIC REQUIRED

See 'Calculate fabric amounts' on facing page for details of how to work out how much fabric and binding you will need.

SUGGESTED FABRICS

Main fabric: sheer fabric such as chiffon, voile or georgette.

Lining and interlining fabric: crepe-back satin or similar. NB As the lining is not pleated and will be pulled tight across the frame, a fabric with a little give would be ideal, such as crepe-back satin. A pale colour is recommended, as it will give the best light.

SEWING NOTIONS

* Thread to match fabric
* Lampshade frame
* Bias binding or cotton tape measuring 1½ times the length of each strut and twice the circumference of the top and bottom rings
* 2 x self-cover buttons to suit the size of your lampshade frame
* Decorative braid measuring the circumference of the bottom ring of the lampshade frame, plus a little extra for turning under

FINISHED SIZE

Depends on the size of the frame

KEY

wrong side of fabric
right side of fabric

A NOTE ON MAKING PLEATS

Pleats work better when they lie along the warp threads of the fabric (the vertical threads, parallel to the selvedge), so bear this in mind when cutting out your pieces.

The total width needed to make the lampshade may be considerably more than the width of your fabric, so you may need to sew one or more pieces together.

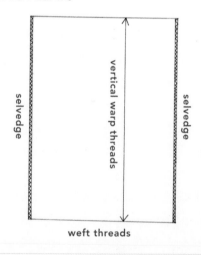

selvedge

vertical warp threads

selvedge

weft threads

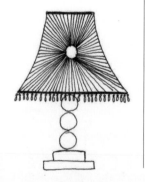

MAIN FABRIC LENGTH

1 To calculate the length of the main fabric, measure from the centre of the front panel of the frame in a straight line across to the point where the side strut and bottom ring meet. Add an extra 2in (5cm) for turnings.

MAIN FABRIC WIDTH

2 To calculate the width required for each half of the frame, add the circumferences of the top and bottom rings together, then divide the answer by two and add twice the height of the frame. Allow 1½ times this measurement.

To calculate the amount of fabric required, divide the total width needed for the lampshade by the width of your fabric and round it up to the nearest whole number. Multiply this by the total length that you require.

LINING AND INTERLINING FABRICS

3 To calculate the fabric required for the lining, measure the circumference of the widest part of the frame, halve it and add an extra 4in (10cm) to give you the width of fabric required. Measure the height of the frame, double it and add an extra 4in (10cm) to give you the length of fabric required. The interlining fabric can be the same colour as the main fabric. Choose a fabric with some give, as with the lining. The amount of fabric required is the same as for the lining.

BINDING

The frame needs to be bound first to provide a foundation to stitch the cover to. This can be done with bias binding or cotton tape. Calculate the amount of binding required by allowing 1½ times the length of each strut and twice the circumference of the top and bottom rings.

TRIMS

Use bias-cut strips from the main fabric to trim your lampshade around the top ring and the two side struts. Allow extra main fabric for this. Alternatively, you can use a purchased braid.

1

2

3

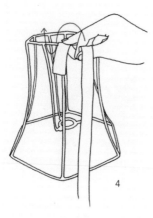

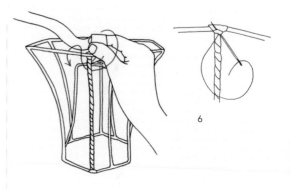

4 Paint the lampshade frame, if necessary, so that the metal doesn't show through the fabric. If using bias binding to cover the frame, open up the folds and press flat to prevent it from becoming too bulky. Starting under the ring at the top of the frame, place the end of the binding against the side strut and wind it around in a figure of eight, over the strut and the top ring, overlapping the end.

6 When you reach the lower end of the strut, turn the lampshade frame upside down and wind the tape in a figure of eight around the bottom ring and the side strut. Hand stitch on the outside of the frame to secure the binding in place. Trim away the end of the tape. Bind the other struts in the same way.

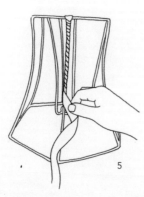

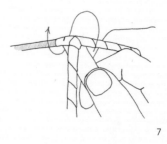

5 Work down to the end of the strut, wrapping the binding around at an angle. Pull on the binding tightly, keeping it smooth, to avoid any creases.

7 Bind the top and bottom rings, winding the binding around each strut in a figure of eight and securing with a few stitches, as before.

Lining

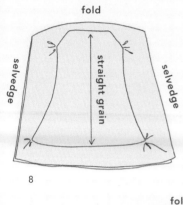

fold

selvedge

straight grain

selvedge

8

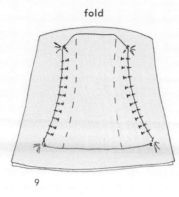

fold

9

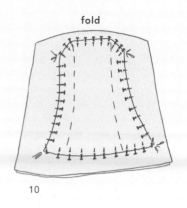

fold

10

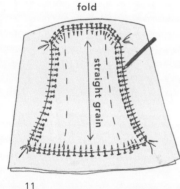

fold

straight grain

11

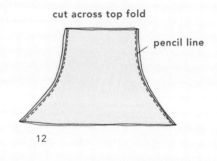

cut across top fold

pencil line

12

8 With right sides together, fold the lining fabric in half and lay it over one half of the frame. The straight grain of the fabric – the warp threads that run parallel to the selvedge – should run from the top to the bottom of the frame.

9 Pin the fabric to the binding at the four points where the side struts meet the top and bottom rings. Smooth the fabric, taking the fullness out, and pin to the side struts with the heads of the pins facing the centre of the lampshade.

10 After pinning the fabric to the struts, pull the fabric tight and pin it to the top and bottom rings, with the points of the pins facing the centre of the lampshade.

11 Insert plenty of extra pins in between those already in the binding of the side struts, easing the fabric until it is smoothed right over the frame. Make sure that the grain of the fabric is straight. Using a soft pencil, mark along the line of pins over each strut.

12 Remove the pins and the fabric from the frame. Pin, then stitch the fabric together just inside the pencil lines, as the lining should be fractionally smaller than the frame itself. Trim the side seams to ¼in (6mm). Cut across the fold line at the top of the fabric.

107

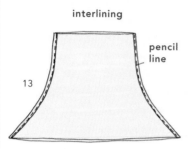

interlining

pencil line

13

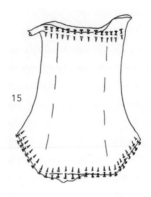

15

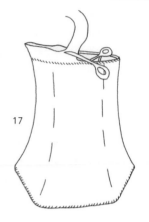

17

13 The interlining is used as a foundation for the pleating. Make the interlining in the same way as the lining, this time stitching just outside the pencil lines to make it a fraction bigger than the frame.

15 Pin the <u>interlining</u> around the top and bottom rings, pulling the fabric taut so that it sits smoothly over the frame.

17 Trim the fabric close to the stitches.

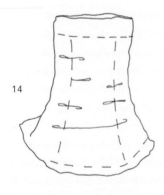

14

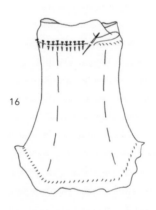

16

14 Pull the interlining over the frame, with the right side on the outside. Position the seams so that they go over the bound side struts.

16 With matching thread, used double, stitch the fabric to the frame by oversewing (see page 152) around the rings.

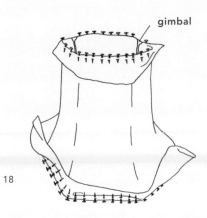

gimbal

18

20

18 With the wrong side facing the struts, slip the lining inside the frame. Position the seams over the inside of the bound struts, matching those of the interlining. Cut small slits in the fabric at the top, so that it sits neatly around the bars of the gimbal (the part of the frame that holds the light fitting). Pull on the lining to keep it taut behind the frame and pin around the top and bottom rings, as for the interlining.

20 To neaten the raw edges around the gimbal bars, cut a 4 x 1in (10 x 2.5cm) piece of lining fabric on the bias for each bar. Turn the long edges in to the centre and press to form a strip about ⅜in (1cm) wide.

21 With the raw edges underneath, slip the strip under the gimbal bar and over the edge of the ring. Pin and stitch in place over the lining stitches on the outside of the lampshade. Trim the ends close to the stitches.

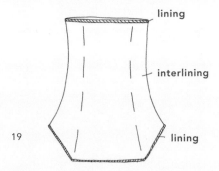

lining

interlining

lining

19

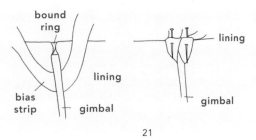

bound ring

lining

lining

bias strip

gimbal

lining

gimbal

21

19 Stitch the lining in place by oversewing around the top and bottom rings, using doubled thread, as before. Work the stitches on the outside of the shade so that they will be concealed by the main fabric covering. Trim the excess fabric close to the stitching.

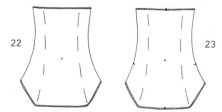

22 Mark the centre point of the front and back panels on the shade. This is the point from which the pleats will radiate on each side.

23 Measure half the circumference of the top ring, down one side strut, halfway around the bottom ring and up the opposite side strut. Divide the measurement by four and mark the shade at the centre point of the top and bottom rings and the points in between the marks just made, on the two side struts.

24 For the first side of the shade, cut the main fabric to the length and width required, joining pieces if necessary. With right sides together, sew the short edges together to form a ring of material, taking a ¼in (6mm) seam allowance.

25 Divide the length of the ring of fabric into quarters and mark the points along one edge. By hand, work two rows of gathering stitches (see page 155), working one row ⅝in (1.5cm) from the unmarked edge and the other ¼in (6mm) inside the first row near the edge. Draw up tightly, forming a circle of fabric. Stitch the gathered edge, with right side facing out, to the marked point in the centre of the lampshade.

26 Smooth the outside edges and match the marked points of the fabric to the marked points of the shade. Pin in place.

27 Starting at the marked point of the bottom ring, begin forming narrow pleats, working in one direction all the way around half of the shade. Pin in position, adjusting the pleats so that they are evenly spaced and face the same way. Hide the joins in the fabric inside a fold. Stitch in place to the rings and struts. Cut away the excess fabric close to the stitching.

28 Finish the other half of the lampshade in the same way, but fold the pleats so that they lie in the opposite direction and match them at the sides.

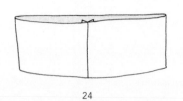

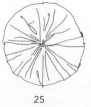

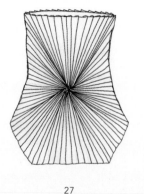

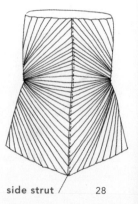

side strut

Trimming

29 The raw edges are covered with bias-cut strips of fabric, although you can use a decorative braid if you prefer. Cut bias strips from the main fabric measuring 1in (2.5cm) wide by the length of each strut. Turn the long edges in to the centre and press. Place the bias strip over the strut, with the raw edges underneath. Sew in place with tiny stitches, working from one side to the other, catching the bias binding to the main cover fabric and then taking the needle behind the binding to the other side.

30 To cover the top ring, prepare bias strip as before. Start ¼in (6mm) behind the top of a side strut. Work around the ring, covering the raw edge. Stitch from side to side as before, taking care not to go through to the inside of the lampshade. Neaten the end by turning it under and overlapping the binding at the side to finish.

31 Starting at a side strut on the bottom ring, trim the end of the decorative braid to neaten and fold under ⅜in (1cm). Pin in place and hand stitch to the ring, covering the raw edges and working from side to side as before. At the other end, turn under ⅜in (1cm), butt the two edges together and slipstitch (see page 151) in place.

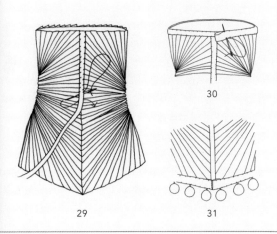

29

30

31

Finishing touches

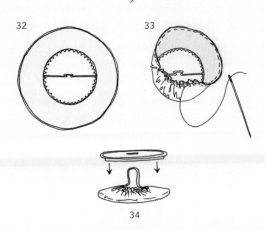

32

33

34

32 Cut one circle to size from the interlining and one or two from the main fabric to cover the button, plus about ½in (12mm) extra all around. Layering the fabrics will prevent the metal of the button from showing through.

33 Lay the main fabric circle(s) over the interlining and run a line of gathering stitches around the edge, stitching through all layers. Place the button dome on the wrong side of the fabric and cover by gathering the circular fabric around it and securing with a few stitches.

34 Slip the button back over the shank, with the ridge facing down. Snap it into place. Cover another button to match the first. Position the covered buttons over the gathered raw edges in the centre panels of the shade and sew in place.

Nº 18

Lounge Suit

Here is the perfect garment to relax in,
with all the allure of a 1940s movie star.
Greta Garbo may have worn similar attire as
she applied her make-up at her dressing table.

❖

ABC DEF

PATTERN PIECES

39 JACKET FRONT
40 JACKET BACK
41 FRONT FACING
42 BACK FACING
43 COLLAR
44 POCKET
45 SLEEVE
46 BELT
47 TROUSER BACK
   (JOIN 47A + 47B)
48 TROUSER FRONT
   (JOIN 48A + 48B)
49 PLACKET

FABRIC REQUIRED

To calculate the length of fabric you need, refer to the appropriate column for your dress size and the fabric width you are using.

FABRIC WIDTH	SMALL	MEDIUM	LARGE
36in (90cm) without nap	5¾yd (5.3m)	5⅞yd (5.4m)	6yd (5.5m)
45in (115cm) without nap	4¾yd (4.4m)	4⅞yd (4.5m)	5yd (4.6m)
60in (150cm) without nap	3¾yd (3.4m)	3⅞yd (3.6m)	4yd (3.7m)
36in (90cm) iron-on interfacing	⅞yd (80cm)	⅞yd (80cm)	1yd (90cm)

SUGGESTED FABRICS Silk crepe-back satin, silk jersey, silk charmeuse, satin, cotton lawn, cotton and silk blend, viscose

SEWING NOTIONS

* Thread to match fabric
* 1⅜yd (1.25m) bias binding, ¾in (2cm) wide
* 5 buttons, approx. ⅜in (1cm) in diameter

KEY

- wrong side of fabric
- right side of fabric
- interfacing

SEAM ALLOWANCES

Take ⅝in (1.5cm) seam allowances throughout, unless otherwise stated

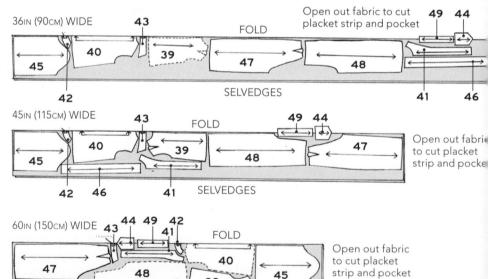

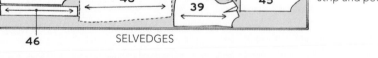

BROKEN LINES INDICATE REVERSE SIDE OF PATTERNS

LOUNGE SUIT JACKET

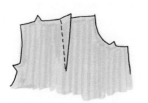

1

Stitch the shoulder darts on the jacket front pieces (see page 154). Press the darts towards the centre fronts (see page 157).

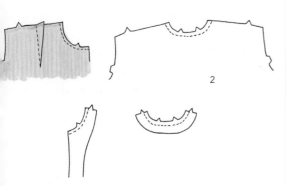

2

Staystitch (see page 152) the neck edges of the front and back jacket pieces and the front and back facings to prevent the fabric from stretching.

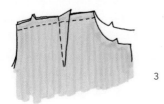

3

With right sides together and matching notches, pin and stitch the front pieces to the back piece at the shoulder seams.

Collar and facings

 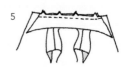

4   Following the manufacturer's instructions, apply iron-on interfacing to the wrong side of one collar piece. This will be the under collar. With right sides together, pin the top collar to this one. Stitch around the three outer edges. Trim the seams and corners and snip the curves (see page 147). Turn right side out and press.

5   With the right side of the under collar to the right side of the garment, matching notches at the front and back neck, pin the neck edges together. Tack the collar in place, stitching through all layers (see page 151).

6   Apply iron-on interfacing to the wrong side of the left and right front facings. Stitch the front facings to the back facing at the shoulder edges. Press the seams open.

7   Turn under and press a ¼in (6mm) hem around the outside edge of the left and right front facings and the back facing. Stitch close to the pressed-under edges.

8   With right sides together, matching notches, pin the facings to the garment. Stitch along the front edges and around the neck. Trim the seam and snip the curves.

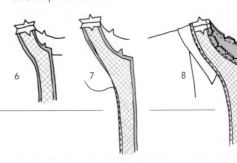

115

Collar and facings

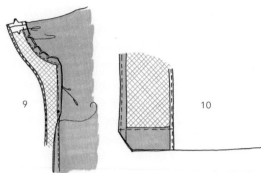

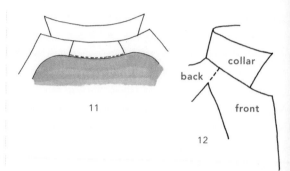

9 Press the seam at the front edges towards the facings. Sew the seam down to the facing, from the dot to the hem, working close to the previous line of stitches.

10 With right sides together, stitch across the lower edge of the front facings, allowing a 1in (2.5cm) hem. Cut diagonally across the corners, taking care not to cut into the stitching.

11 Turn right side out and press. Press the back facing to the inside of the garment. Pin the lower, turned edge of the facing to the inside back, then tack and stitch in place in between the shoulder seams, either by hand or by machine.

12 On the right side of the garment, run a line of stitches by hand or machine along the shoulder seam line to catch the facings down.

Pocket

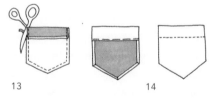

13 Press under ¼in (6mm) along the top edge of the pocket. Turn the top edge to the outside of the pocket along the fold line to form the facing. Stitch along the seam line along the side and bottom edges. Trim the seams to ¼in (6mm).

14 Turn the facing to the inside. Turn under the raw edges along the stitch line from the previous step and press. Tack the facing down, close to the turned edge. Topstitch (see page 152) along the tacking line, then remove the tacking stitches.

15 Pin the pocket to the right side of the left front, matching the dots. Tack and then stitch in place, stitching close to the side and lower edges.

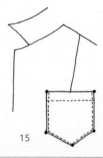

Sleeves and side seams

16 Run two rows of gathering stitches (see page 155) in between the notches, by hand or using a long machine stitch, working one row along the seam line and the other ¼in (6mm) inside the seam line, to ease the fullness of the top of the sleeve.

17 With right sides together, pin the sleeve to the armhole, aligning the centre dot with the shoulder seam. Match notches and seam lines at the underarms. Pull up the gathering stitches to fit. Tack the sleeve in place, easing in the fullness. Stitch the underarm seams, then work a second line of stitches close to the first for added strength. Trim each side of the seam allowance separately, from the underarm to the notch. Press the seam towards the sleeve.

18 Stitch the sleeve and side seams, matching notches and underarm seams.

19 Turn under and press ¼in (6mm) on the lower edge of the sleeve. Turn up the hem and press. Stitch close to the turned edge.

20 Turn under and press ¼in (6mm) on the hem, tucking it under behind the front facings. Turn up the hem and press. Stitch close to the pressed edge, working right across the front facings to the end.

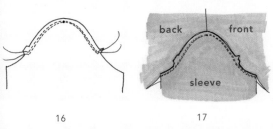

16

17

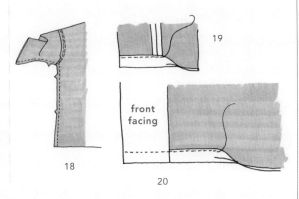

18

19

20

Buttons and buttonholes

21 Work four buttonholes (see pages 160–1) on the right front, as indicated on the pattern. Lap the right front over the left, matching the centre front. Mark the position of buttons to correspond with the buttonholes. Attach the buttons to the left front.

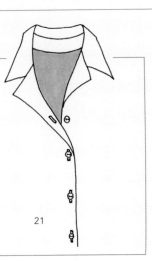

21

117

 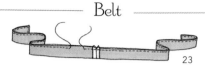 

22 Stitch the short edges of the two belt pieces to make one long length. Press the seam open.

23 Fold the piece in half lengthways, right sides together, and stitch around the unfolded edges, leaving a 4in (10cm) opening in the long edge. Trim the seam allowance and cut diagonally across the corners, taking care not to cut the stitching.

24 Turn the belt right side out and press. Work a line of topstitching all around, close to the edges.

25 To make the loops to carry the belt, cut two pieces of fabric measuring 3in (8cm) long by 1in (2.5cm) wide. Turn under ¼in (6mm) at the short edges, turn the long edges in to the centre and press.

26 Fold the strip in half lengthways and stitch along the long edge, near the edge.

27 Turn under ⅜in (1cm) at the short ends and stitch in place at the side seams, as indicated by the dots on the pattern.

  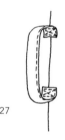

LOUNGE SUIT TROUSERS

1 Stitch the darts (see page 154) in the trouser backs and press towards the centre backs.

2 To make the pleats in the trouser fronts, fold the fabric along the solid lines. Tack along the broken lines. Stitch down the tacking line from the waist for 1½in (4cm). Press the pleats towards the side seams.

3 With right sides together, matching notches, stitch the right front and back leg pieces together along the side seam. Repeat with the left front and back leg pieces, leaving an opening from the waist to the first notch on the left trouser leg for the fastening. Press the seam open.

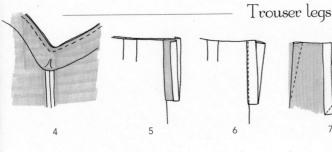

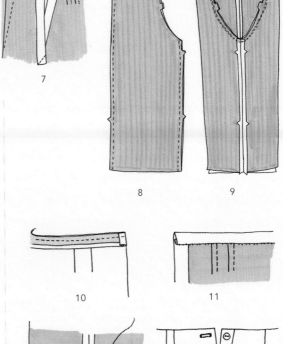

4 With the right side of the placket strip to the wrong side of the left trouser leg opening, pin and stitch the placket strip down one side of the opening and up the other. Trim the seam and press towards the placket strip.

5 Turn under and press ⅝in (1.5cm) on the other side of the placket strip.

6 Fold the strip so that the pressed edge meets the line of stitching on the right side of the trouser leg. Pin and slipstitch by hand (see page 151) or machine stitch in place.

7 Turn in the piece on the front edge to form the facing and then tack in place at the waist. Leave the back edge of placket at the outside of the garment. Stitch a diagonal line at the fold to prevent it from turning to the outside.

8 With right sides together, matching the notches, stitch the inside leg seams.

9 With right sides together, matching the notches at the front and back, slip one leg inside the other. Pin and stitch from the front waist, across the leg seams and up to the back waist. It is best to work a second row of stitches over the first on this seam for added strength. Turn the trousers right side out.

10 Open out one edge of the bias binding and, with right sides together, pin and stitch the creased line of the binding to the waist, turning under the raw edges at the side opening.

11 Trim the seam and press the bias binding to the inside. Slipstitch the bias binding in place on the inside of the waist.

12 Turn under 1in (2.5cm) at the hem and press. Turn the raw edge under and press, then stitch the hem.

13 Work a buttonhole (see pages 160–1) at the opening of the front waist, as indicated on the pattern. Sew a button to the back waist to correspond with the buttonhole.

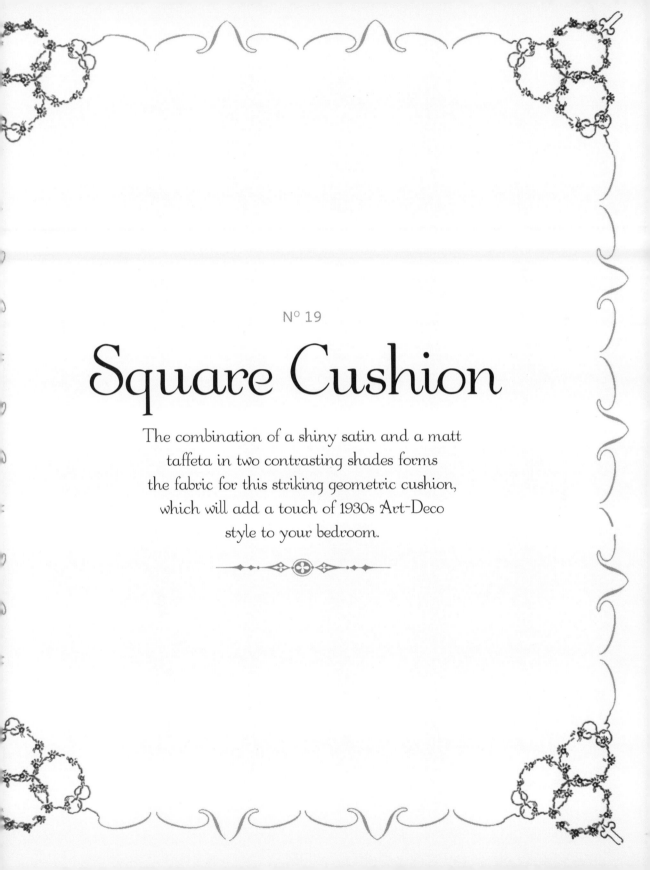

Square Cushion

The combination of a shiny satin and a matt
taffeta in two contrasting shades forms
the fabric for this striking geometric cushion,
which will add a touch of 1930s Art-Deco
style to your bedroom.

FABRIC REQUIRED

1yd (90cm) each of 2 contrasting shades, 45in (115cm) wide

SUGGESTED FABRICS Silk dupion, silk shantung, silk charmeuse, satin, crepe, taffeta

SEWING NOTIONS

* Thread to match main fabric
* 2¼yd (2.1m) satin bias binding, ¾in (2cm) wide
* 2¼yd (2.1m) piping cord
* 20 x 20in (50 x 50cm) cushion pad
* 2 self-cover buttons, 1½in (38mm) in diameter
* 2in (5cm) elastic, ¼in (6mm) wide
* Large-eyed sharp needle

SEAM ALLOWANCES

Take ⅝in (1.5cm) seam allowances throughout unless otherwise stated

FINISHED SIZE

20 x 20in (50 x 50cm), excluding piping

Preparing the fabric

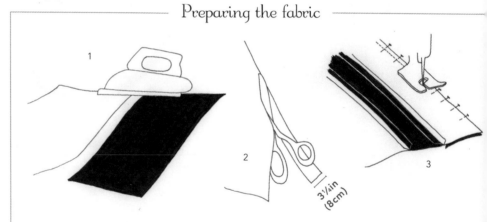

1   Iron the fabric to ensure the strips will be perfectly straight and easy to cut.

2   Working across the width of the fabric, measure and cut both fabrics into strips 3¼in (8cm) deep. This includes seam allowances of ⅝in (1.5cm) on each side. Take care to make each strip of fabric the same width, so that they match when they are joined to form the cushion cover.

3   With right sides together, alternating the colours, pin and stitch the strips together to produce a striped fabric. Trim the seams and press the seam allowances to one side.

Joining the pattern pieces

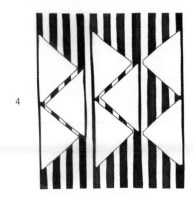

4

5

6

Attaching the piping

7 Open up the folded edges of the binding and wrap around the piping cord. Using a zipper foot on the sewing machine, stitch along the binding as close to the cord as possible.

8 Starting at a corner, aligning the raw edges of the binding with the edge of the cushion, pin and tack the bound piping around the edges of the right side of one cushion piece. Ease the binding around the corners and overlap the ends, folding the raw edge under, to neaten the join. Sew in place using a zipper foot.

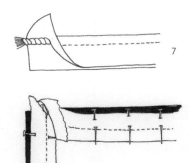

7

8

4 Make eight copies of the quarter pattern piece and use these to cut eight identical triangular pieces from the prepared fabric, taking care to position the stripes in the same place on each piece.

5 With right sides together, matching the stripes, pin and stitch the diagonal edges of two quarters together at a time. You will have four right-angled triangles. Press the seams open.

6 With right sides together, matching the stripes and centre seams, pin and stitch the right-angled triangles together in pairs to complete the front and back of the cushion. Trim the seams and press the seams open (see page 157).

Joining the front and back pieces

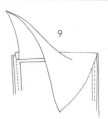

9 With right sides together, pin and tack the front and back cushion pieces together around the edges, keeping the piping to the inside.

10 Starting three-quarters of the way across one edge, stitch the pieces together using the line of stitching made when attaching the piping as a guide. Finish one-quarter of the way across the first edge, leaving an opening of about 10in (25cm). Trim the seam and cut diagonally across the corners (see page 147).

11 Turn right side out and press.

12 Turn under ⅝in (1.5cm) at open edge and press. Insert the cushion pad into the striped cover.

13 Now pin and slipstitch (see page 151) the opening closed.

Finishing touches

14 Cut a circle of fabric to size to cover the button, plus about ½in (12mm) extra all around.

15 Many self-cover buttons have teeth to hook the fabric onto; if yours do not, run a line of gathering stitches (see page 155) by hand around the edge of the fabric. Place the button dome on the wrong side of the fabric and cover the sides by hooking the material onto the teeth or gathering up the circular fabric around it, and secure with a few stitches.

16 Slip the button back over the shank, with the ridge facing down. Snap it into place. Cover another button to match the first.

17 Sew a button securely to one end of the elastic.

18 With a long needle, thread the other end of the elastic through the centre of the cushion to the other side. Stretching the elastic, sew the remaining button securely to the free end.

'Like charity, I believe glamour
should begin at home.'

LORETTA YOUNG

Sleep Mask

The perfect accessory when taking a siesta,
this sleep mask will add glamour to your
40 winks and help bring sweet dreams. A pretty
stretch ribbon keeps it on your sleepy head.

FABRIC REQUIRED

Main fabric: 9½ x 6in (24 x 15cm)
Lining fabric: 9½ x 6in (24 x 15cm)
Wadding: 9½ x 6in (24 x 15cm)
Tulle: 60 x 2¾in (150 x 7cm)

SUGGESTED FABRICS

Silk satin, silk crepe-back satin, polyester satin for both the main and lining fabrics

SEWING NOTIONS

* Thread to match fabric
* Dressmaker's carbon paper
* Stranded black embroidery thread
* Embroidery needle
* Two 21in (53cm) lengths of stretch ribbon, approx. ¼in (6mm) wide

SEAM ALLOWANCES

Take ⅝in (1.5cm) seam allowances throughout unless otherwise stated

FINISHED SIZE

7½in (19cm) wide, excluding trim

KEY

wrong side of fabric
right side of fabric

Embroidery

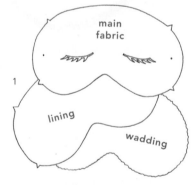

1 Enlarge the template on page 170 by 320% and cut out. Cut one pattern piece each in main fabric, lining and wadding. Transfer the eyelashes to the main fabric by slipping dressmaker's carbon paper between the pattern and the right side of the fabric and tracing over the design with a pencil.

2 Using two strands of black embroidery thread, embroider the eyelashes by first working a chain stitch along the eye line and then embroidering over the chain stitch with satin stitch (see pages 164–5). This will create a raised line of stitching as well as a neater finish.

3 Work the lashes in satin stitch, following the carbon lines and keeping the stitches close together.

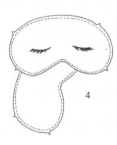

Staystitch (see page 152) around
the embroidered satin and
the lining ⅛in (3mm) from the
outside edges.

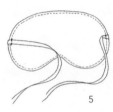

5 With the wrong side of the
ribbon to the right side of
the lining, tack the ribbons
in place as indicated by the
dots on the pattern.

6 Join the short ends of the strip
of tulle together to form a ring
and press the seam open (see
page 157). Now, with wrong
sides together, fold the strip in
half lengthways and then press.

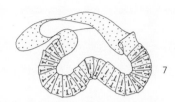

7 Aligning the raw edges of the
tulle with the edge of the right
side of the lining, form the tulle
into evenly spaced pleats to fit
around the lining by folding the
doubled fabric and laying the
folds so that they face the same
direction. Pin the pleats down as
you go and then tack (see page
151) in place, taking care to
ease them around the curves.

8 Place the wadding on your work
surface, with the lining right side
up on top and the embroidered
satin right side down on top of
the lining, keeping the tulle and
ribbons sandwiched inside. Pin
and stitch together, leaving an
opening at the top edge. Trim
the seam and notch the curves
(see page 147).

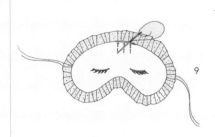

9 Turn right side out. Turn under
the seam allowances at the
opening and slipstitch (see page
151) together to join.

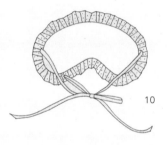

10 Press lightly with a cool iron.
Tie the ends of the stretch
ribbon in a bow to fit the head.

HONE YOUR
SKILLS

Sewing Tools

A few essential tools and a basic knowledge
of needlework is all that is needed to achieve
a beautifully finished handmade garment
or item for the home.

SCISSORS

Tailor's and dressmaking shears have long blades and should be kept sharp for ease of cutting. They must be kept solely for cutting fabric; use a separate pair of scissors for cutting paper patterns.

A small pair of very sharp pointed scissors is essential for cutting threads and it can also be useful for fiddly tasks such as unpicking stitches.

Buttonhole scissors are useful because they are made specifically for the job, with short, sharp-pointed blades to cut the fabric. They often have an adjustable screw so that the buttonhole can be cut to the size required.

Pinking shears are perfect for finishing seams, as the jagged blades cut a zig-zag line that prevents the fabric from fraying. They should be kept for fabric only, as cutting paper will blunt the blades.

PINS

Pins come in various sizes, for use on fine laces to heavy woven cloth; ones with coloured glass heads are easy to find in fabric. Take care not to use pins that are rusty or blunt, as this will damage the fabric.

TAPE MEASURE

A tape measure is a vital piece of equipment for dressmaking. A PVC tape is preferable, as it won't stretch or tear like a fabric or paper one.

THIMBLE

A thimble should fit comfortably, without falling off, protecting the finger that pushes the needle through the fabric.

MARKING TOOLS

Tailor's chalk is used for marking pattern shapes on fabric and can be brushed away. It comes in white for use on dark cloth and in various colours for use on light fabric. It should be kept sharp for a clean line. The chalk can also be found in the form of a pencil.

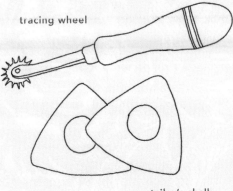

tracing wheel

tailor's chalk

A tracing wheel is mainly used for marking and duplicating lines on paper patterns and transferring pattern lines to fabric. It has a finely spiked wheel with very sharp points that will not tear the paper. The wheels should not be used on silks, as the spikes can tear the fine threads of the fabric.

Dressmaker's carbon paper is used in the same way as the traditional stationery kind, for copying documents. It is heavier, making it easy to pin to a fabric without tearing, and is available in yellow, white, blue and red, to work with light and dark fabrics.

NEEDLES

Needles are available in an array of sizes for a multitude of needlework tasks. Make sure they are not rusty and the points are sharp so as not to damage the fabric. The needle should go through the fabric with ease, without leaving a mark or hole.

HAND-STITCHING NEEDLES

'Sharps' are used for general sewing and come in various sizes to suit different weights of fabric. They have quite a large eye, which makes threading easier. 'Betweens' are short, slim needles with a narrow eye, ideal for working small, even stitches. There are also needles specifically for darning, embroidery, quilting, beading and millinery.

MACHINE NEEDLES

It is important to use the right size needle for the weight of fabric to produce the best results. Universal needles have a slightly rounded point for use with knitted fabrics but they are sharp enough to go through woven fabrics. For knitted fabrics, a ballpoint needle slips between the fibres of the fabric, preventing snagging. There are also needles specifically for use with denim and leather, and twin needles, used for working two even rows of stitching.

Needle sizes are shown in both imperial and metric. The smallest sizes relate to the finest needles for use with lightweight fabrics. Where the number is larger, the needle is bigger, for sewing medium-to-heavyweight material.

MACHINE NEEDLE SIZE GUIDE

SIZE	FABRIC EXAMPLES
8/60	Sheer fabrics, chiffon, georgette
10/70	Lining fabrics, cotton lawn
11/80	Shirting fabrics, lightweight cotton
14/90	Cotton sateen, linen
16/100	Denim, canvas
18/110	Leather, vinyl, upholstery fabrics

SEWING MACHINE

Many modern sewing machines have a huge variety of stitch selections. However, all the projects in this book can be easily made with a fairly basic machine that does straight and zig-zag stitch and has a zipper foot. A lot of machines offer automatic buttonholing; this is very useful but not vital, as even an old treadle or hand-operated sewing machine can be used and, if zig-zag stitch is not available, the buttonholes (see pages 160–1) can be worked by hand.

CARE OF THE MACHINE

Regular maintenance of your sewing machine is essential to keep it running smoothly. Always unplug it before cleaning and oiling. Lint (a combination of fabric and thread particles) gets caught up near the bobbin and in hidden areas, and should be removed before it causes problems with the machine.

Use proper sewing-machine oil and refer to the manual for the areas that need oiling. Tighten all the screws and then work some machine stitches on scraps of fabric so that any excess oil runs onto that, rather than onto your next sewing project.

USING THE MACHINE

Have your machine set up in an area with plenty of light and where you can be comfortably seated. Before sewing, make sure that the machine is threaded correctly and that the two threads, from the needle and bobbin, are placed towards the back of the work. Turn the wheel towards you so that the needle is in the work, preventing a tangle of threads. Every time you begin a new project or use a different type of stitch, practise first on a spare piece of fabric to check the tension and avoid having to unpick mistakes.

Taking it slowly will ensure control of the machine and problems with the tension or tangling threads will be less likely.

Fabric & Threads

There is a vast array of fabulous fabrics
out there, waiting to be discovered
and turned into a garment or home
accessory. Likewise, the many colourful
threads available can turn your plain
stitching into an eye-catching statement.

CHOOSING FABRICS

Often, it is finding a fabric that first sparks an idea for a design: a pattern, print, colour or texture will catch your eye and a concept will form. Remnants can be used for small projects for the wardrobe or home, or can form a detail on a garment, such as a pocket, collar or corsage.

Vintage finds are exciting, as the pattern will no longer be widely available and as a result you will have something quite unique.

Make sure that the structure of the fabric is strong enough for what you plan, as old material can perish, disintegrating in the wash or with handling. Work around faded patches, stains or holes and this long-forgotten treasure will be revived and cherished in its new form.

Recycled clothes and linens that you no longer wear or use, as well as charity-shop and boot-fair finds, are another rich source for fabrics and haberdashery. Buttons and lace can be removed and reused, and the fabric can be transformed.

When shopping for a particular project, the pattern requirements are important. Consider the fabric's weight and texture, and how it drapes and gathers. Check that the material is suitable for its intended use. If it is for a garment, will it complement your complexion and how will it wear? Fabric care should also be considered.

PREPARING FABRIC

It is advisable to launder washable fabrics before use so that any shrinkage occurs before the item is made up. Always iron the fabric to ensure the pattern is cut accurately, as this will affect the finished piece. Make sure that your iron is set to the right heat for the fabric type. It is vital that the grain of the fabric is straight before you start, as the direction of the grain will greatly affect the way the finished garment hangs. Make sure that the warp and weft (vertical and horizontal) threads are always at right angles to each other.

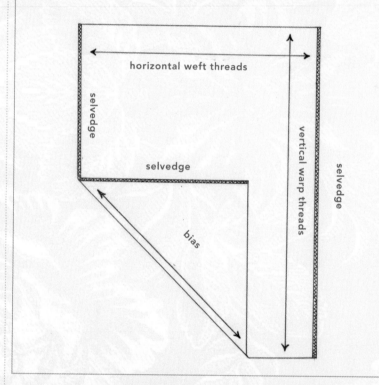

PREPARING FABRIC

horizontal weft threads

selvedge

selvedge

vertical warp threads

selvedge

bias

STRAIGHTENING THE FABRIC

Straighten the weft edges (the horizontal threads that lie between the selvedges) by clipping the fabric at a selvedge edge and tearing it across, or by withdrawing a thread from the fabric and cutting along the straight line it produces.

Straighten the fabric by stretching on the bias or crossway until the edges lie together.

'Luxury must be comfortable,
otherwise it is not luxury.'

COCO CHANEL

INTERFACING

Interfacing adds structure to an area of a garment, such as setting collars and smoothing lapels and front edges. It is available in light, medium or heavy weights, to match the weight of the fabric you are using, and comes in black or charcoal grey for dark fabrics and white for light shades of fabric.

There are three main weaves available in interfacing. Woven interfacing has a grain that should be matched with the grain of the fabric that is to be interfaced. Non-woven interfacing can be cut in any direction as it has no grain, making it more economical than woven interfacing. Knit interfacing has a stretch to it for use with knitted fabrics. The two main types of interfacing are sew-in and iron-on.

SEW-IN INTERFACING
This type of interfacing is stitched to the fabric to hold it and is used on material that is heat sensitive or open weave and unsuitable for iron-on interfacing. It is also good when a softer drape is desired.

IRON-ON INTERFACING
This type of facing has a shiny, fusible side, which is laid on top of the wrong side of the fabric. It is a good idea to test it out on a scrap of material first to check that the weight you are using is correct.

Make sure the iron is at the right temperature for the fabric. Place a damp cloth over the pieces and press the iron down for a few seconds, then lift and repeat on another area.

Do not drag the iron over the fabric, as it could pucker or move the material. After the interfacing has been fused in place, allow the fabric to cool before stitching.

THREADS
There is a vast choice of shades available to match the fabric chosen for your sewing project. When matching the colour, find a thread that is slightly darker on the reel as it will look lighter when worked into the fabric. Choose a strong thread for sewing seams. Vintage threads, with their fading colours, are beautiful but may break easily; these threads are better used for hand finishing, adding an authentic vintage touch.

Tacking thread is cheaper and as the stitches are temporary, will break easily – perfect for the task, but not ideal for sewing permanent seams.

Embroidery threads with their jewel colours are available in a wide range of shades and the strands can be divided to produce finer stitches.

When sewing on the machine, use the same thread on the bobbin as in the needle. If you are stitching a dark ribbon to a light fabric, the colour on the bobbin and needle can be changed to match, but don't mix the fibres.

Garment Sizes

The garment patterns in this book have
been designed for a comfortable fit,
allowing extra fabric for wearing ease.

Patterns are in small, medium and large sizes.
To help choose the correct size, please refer to the chart below.

DRESS SIZE	SMALL	MEDIUM	LARGE
Bust	32–34in (82–87cm)	36–38in (92–97cm)	40–42in (102–107cm)
Waist	24–26in (61–66cm)	28–30in (71–76cm)	32–34in (81–86cm)
Hips	35–37in (89–94cm)	39–41in (99–104cm)	43–45in (109–114cm)

TAKING MEASUREMENTS

When taking width measurements, make sure that the tape is parallel
to the floor and held taut, but not tight, against the body.

BUST: Measure over the fullest part of the bust and straight across the back.

WAIST: Tie a length of string or ribbon around your waist to find your natural waistline and measure over the string or ribbon.

HIPS: Measure around the fullest part of the hip, which on average is around 9in (23cm) below the waistline.

BACK WAIST LENGTH: Measure from the neck bone, down the centre back, to the waist.

SKIRT LENGTH: Measure from centre back waist to the desired length.

The following measurements are useful when making trousers:

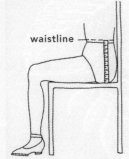

waistline

Crotch length: Sit on a hard, flat chair and measure from the side of the waist to the seat of the chair. To check your crotch measurement against that of the pattern, measure near the side seam from the widest part of the crotch to the waist.

The measurement should match your own with ½–1in (12mm–2.5cm) extra allowed for sitting ease.

Leg: Take this measurement at the side, from the waistline to the floor or to the desired trouser length.

Understanding Patterns

Follow the directions on the paper patterns,
taking time to transfer all the necessary
markings to the prepared fabric before
you start to sew.

PATTERN MARKINGS

The diagrams on the patterns show how the pattern is to be laid on the fabric and where the cutting and sewing lines are, as well as features such as the position of pockets and darts.

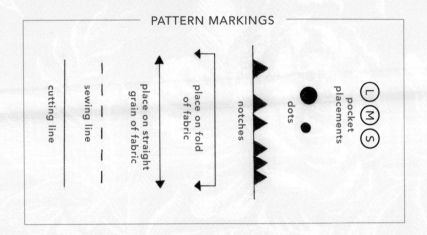

PATTERN MARKINGS

cutting line · sewing line · place on straight grain of fabric · place on fold of fabric · notches · dots · pocket placements · L M S

CUTTING LINE
The cutting line is a continuous line on the pattern.

SEWING LINE
The sewing line is indicated by a broken line. The seam allowances are ⅝in (1.5cm) unless otherwise stated on the pattern.

GRAIN LINES
When laying out the pattern on the fabric make sure that the line of the grain, which is marked by a long, double-ended arrow, follows the selvedge of the fabric. Some pattern pieces need to be placed on a fold, which is indicated by the arrows at an angle to the grain line. Fold the fabric horizontally and place the fold line on the pattern against that of the fabric.

NOTCHES
The notches are used to indicate the parts of the pattern pieces that need to be aligned when they are sewn together. Where there are two or more notches together on a pattern, cut them in blocks for ease, rather than individually. Match the notches with those of the same number on the piece to be joined.

DOTS
Dots refer to points that should meet on pattern pieces or show where a line of stitching should begin or end.

POCKET PLACEMENTS
A set of circles mark each corner or point of where a pocket should be placed.

LAYING OUT THE PATTERN

Where applicable, follow the cutting layout for the width of the fabric you have chosen. This appears at the beginning of each project. Each pattern piece is numbered so it can be easily identified on the cutting layout. The broken lines indicate the reverse side of the pattern pieces, so should be placed with the right side facing down on the fabric. Where the lines of the pattern pieces in the cutting layout are continuous, these should be placed right side up on the fabric.

For double thickness, fold the fabric with right sides together and lay the pattern pieces on the wrong side.

For single thickness, lay the pattern pieces on the right side of the fabric.

When more than one of the same piece is to be cut one at a time, reverse the paper pattern for the second piece.

NAP

The nap is a pile produced by directional raised fibres on fabrics such as velvet. Fabrics with a pile or a one-way pattern must be cut with all the pattern pieces placed facing the same direction. The yardage/meterage required in this book is for fabrics without nap, so you should allow for extra if you choose a fabric with nap or a one-way design. When working with a nap, the pattern should be pinned to the wrong side of the fabric before cutting.

The direction of the pile can be found by brushing your hand over the material. Brushing with the direction of the nap will feel smooth, whereas brushing against the nap will feel rough. A shiny, silky look is produced when the nap is running down. When the nap is running up, the fabric shade is deeper and richer.

CUTTING OUT PATTERN PIECES

Pin the pattern pieces to the fabric so that the pins lie in the same direction and do not obstruct the cutting line. Use enough pins to hold the pattern down, taking care not to pucker the fabric.

Using sharp scissors, place one hand flat on the pattern and fabric to hold it down, keeping it flat so that the lines being cut are accurate.

Cut away from you along the seam line – the solid lines of the pattern. Cut notches outwards, rather than into the seam allowance.

ADJUSTING A PATTERN

Check that the measurements given for the pattern you are using correspond with your own (see Garment Sizes, page 139). Take into account the extra allowed for ease of fit. The garments are designed for a comfortable fit, though you may wish to adjust the length.

'A woman is closest to being naked when she is well dressed.'

COCO CHANEL

LENGTHENING A PATTERN

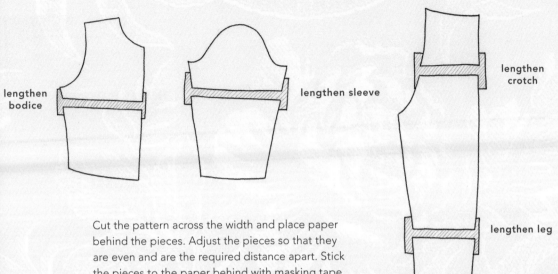

lengthen
bodice

lengthen sleeve

lengthen
crotch

lengthen leg

Cut the pattern across the width and place paper
behind the pieces. Adjust the pieces so that they
are even and are the required distance apart. Stick
the pieces to the paper behind with masking tape
or sticky tape. Trim the excess paper from each side.

SHORTENING A PATTERN

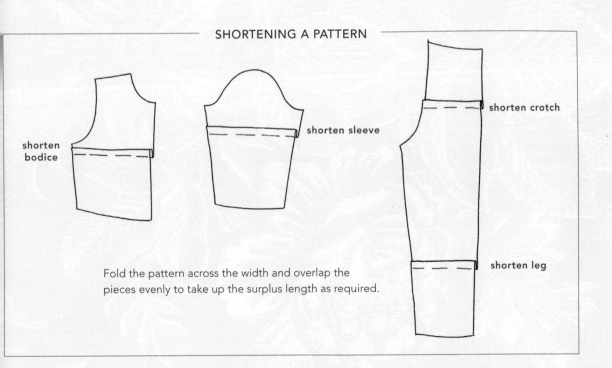

shorten
bodice

shorten sleeve

shorten crotch

shorten leg

Fold the pattern across the width and overlap the
pieces evenly to take up the surplus length as required.

Pattern Sheets

Each pattern piece is numbered so it can be
easily identified from the list given at the
beginning of each project, and found on
the pattern sheets at the back of the book.

HOW TO FIND THE PATTERNS

Select the pattern pieces for the project you are making. These are listed at the beginning of each project and can be found on the pattern sheets, A–F, at the back of the book. The pattern pieces for each particular project are colour coded, such as the nightdress (see below right), which is in orange, and numbered, so they can be easily found within the pattern sheets.

COPYING PATTERNS

The pattern pieces on the enclosed pattern sheets are printed in actual size, ready to be copied or traced. The patterns can be traced onto dressmaker's tissue paper, or tracing paper, which is available in rolls.

For more durable patterns, you may want to transfer the pieces to a heavier paper or cardstock. Slip dressmaker's carbon paper, carbon side down, between the pattern sheets and the paper or card and trace over the chosen pattern pieces with a pencil or tracing wheel.

Another way to copy the patterns is by taking them to a copy shop to be printed. They can also be photocopied, although some pieces may need to be taped together if they are larger than the copier paper size.

Make sure the patterns are laid flat so they don't distort when printed. Check you have every pattern piece required before you start the project

and that you have transferred all the pattern markings (see page 141), ready to use.

CUTTING OUT YOUR SIZE

The garment patterns are in three sizes: small, medium and large. To calculate the size you need, refer to page 139 for how to take your measurements and, based on those measurements, decide which will be the correct size of pattern to cut out.

Each size is labelled along the cutting lines with 'S' for small, 'M' for medium and 'L' for large. When tracing or cutting the photocopied pattern pieces, follow the lines according to your size.

JOINING PIECES

Some of the longer pattern pieces, such as the nightdress back, will need joining before laying out on the fabric. These are indicated by the dotted lines. Cut carefully along the line of one piece and allow a little extra paper, around ⅝–1in (1.5–2.5cm), beyond the line of the other.

Join the pieces by lapping them, matching the dotted lines and arrows, and taping them together with masking tape or sticky tape.

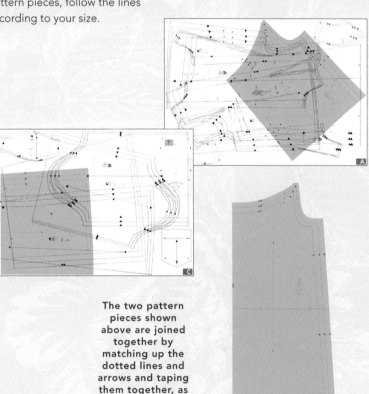

The two pattern pieces shown above are joined together by matching up the dotted lines and arrows and taping them together, as seen on the right.

Seams

The seam is the line of stitching
that produces the structure
and shape of the article, creating
a three-dimensional form from
the cut pieces of fabric.

PINNING SEAMS

If you are a beginner, pinning and tacking seams are very useful to ensure that the fabric will not slip about when stitching. Then you will be able to produce a neat seam and avoid mistakes. As your confidence builds with experience, you may feel you no longer need to pin seams before you stitch.

PINNING FABRIC ALONG THE SEAM LINE

Insert the pins so that the point faces away from you. As the pins cannot be stitched over when in line with the needle, they will be easy to remove with the pin heads facing towards you; you will also avoid pricking your finger.

STITCHING OVER PINS

Pins can be machine stitched over when they are at right angles to the edge of the work. This way, the needle will not get broken by hitting the pins and they can be removed after stitching the seam.

FLAT SEAM

The patterns in this book use a flat seam unless otherwise stated. With right sides of fabric together, stitch along the ⅝in (1.5cm) seam line and press the seam open. To secure the line of stitching and prevent the stitches from unravelling, run the machine backwards and then forwards over the first and last few stitches. The raw edges of the seam can be trimmed to neaten it.

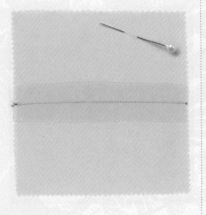

CLIPPING SEAMS

Where a seam is curved, clipping or cutting notches into the fabric will enable it to lie flat. On fabrics that fray easily, cut the layers of the seams separately and make sure that the snips and notches of each seam do not match. To reduce bulk in heavier fabrics, seams can be layered so that they lie flat by cutting one side of the seam allowance slightly smaller than the other.

For those that curve outwards, cut a V-shape into the seam close to the stitch line. For inward curves, snip a straight line in the seam close to the stitches.

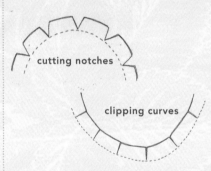

cutting notches

clipping curves

TRIMMING CORNERS

Corners should be trimmed to an angle so that the fabric lies flat when the work is turned right side out. An inverted corner should be snipped close to the seam line.

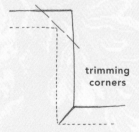

trimming corners

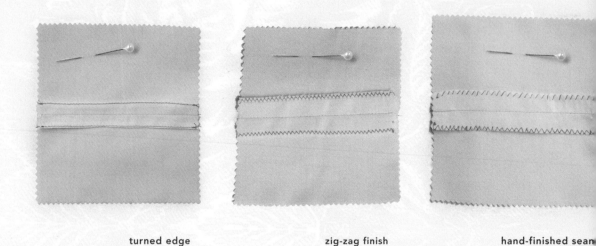

turned edge   zig-zag finish   hand-finished seam

SEAM FINISHES

For a couture finish, the look of the inside of a garment is as important as the outside. Finishing the seams will neaten the garment and prevent fraying, therefore making it more durable. All the seams on the projects in this book should be finished as they are stitched, by using any of the following methods.

TURNED EDGE

Turn under the raw edges of the seam and stitch close to the fold.

ZIG-ZAG FINISH

Work a line of zig-zag stitches close to the raw edges of the seam (see page 152). Practise on a scrap of fabric beforehand to achieve the desired stitch length and width.

HAND-FINISHED SEAM

Neaten the edges with oversewing (see page 152), taking care not to work the stitches too tightly, as this will cause the edges to curl. Work diagonal stitches evenly, wrapping them over the edge of the seam. For fabrics that are prone to fraying, work along the same line of stitches in the opposite direction, creating a zig-zag effect.

SPECIAL SEAMS

The following seams are ideal for lingerie. They produce a neat finish
and are hard wearing, especially as the items will be regularly laundered.

FELL SEAM

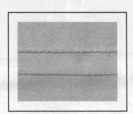

In a fell seam, the stitching forms a decorative seam
that is visible on the right side of the fabric. It is used
for lingerie but is also suitable for heavier garments,
such as jeans and outerwear.

1   With wrong sides of fabric together, stitch along
    the ⅝in (1.5cm) seam line and press it to one side.

2   Trim the lower-edge seam allowance to ⅛in
    (3mm). Turn under and press ¼in (6mm) on the
    raw edge of the other seam allowance.

3   Press the wider seam allowance over the narrow,
    trimmed edge and stitch down, close to the fold,
    encasing the raw edge. This seam is finished on
    the right side of the fabric. Where the seam is
    curved, a French seam (see right) is more suitable.

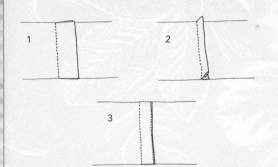

FRENCH SEAM

Where the pattern states that the right sides of
the fabric should be together to sew the seam,
start a French seam with the wrong sides of the
fabric together.

1   Stitch the first seam with wrong sides together,
    working ¼in (6mm) from the seam line.

2   Press the seam to one side, then turn the work
    to the inside and press.

3   With right sides together, stitch along the
    seam allowance to encase the first seam.
    When a French seam is stitched on a curved
    line, snip the first seam to allow it to expand
    around the curve so that it sits flat inside the
    second line of stitches.

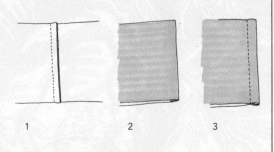

Hand & Machine Stitching

Hand stitching became less of a necessity with the introduction of the sewing machine, but it has since become a mark of luxury, with the attention to detail defining the quality. Machine stitching, however, is stronger and quicker than sewing by hand.

HAND STITCHING

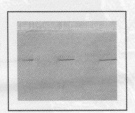

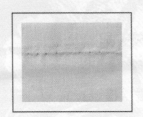

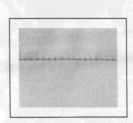

TACKING STITCH

These are the temporary stitches used to join pieces of fabric ready for fitting and permanent stitching. They are the easiest and quickest hand-sewn stitch. Knot the end of the thread and work large stitches from right to left. Finish with a couple of stitches worked over each other to secure the end. When the seam has been permanently sewn by machine or hand, remove the tacking stitches.

SLIPSTITCH

This stitch produces an almost invisible finish and is used for hemming and attaching trimmings. Pass the needle through the folded edge and, at the same point, pick up a thread or two of the fabric underneath. Continue in this way, spacing the stitches evenly around ⅛–¼in (3–6mm) apart.

HEM STITCH

Bring the thread through to the edge of the folded hem. Pick up a thread of fabric and pass the needle diagonally through the edge of the hem. Continue in this way, spacing the stitches around ¼in (6mm) apart.

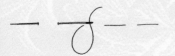

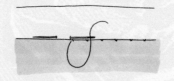

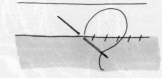

LADDER STITCH

This stitch is for joining two adjacent edges and is used to close the open ends neatly of the powder puff (see page 15). Working on the right side of the fabric, make a stitch at the seam line of one side of the opening and then work a stitch in the other side. After two or three stitches, pull to close. The stitches will be practically invisible and the seam will be hidden inside.

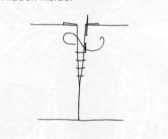

OVERSEWING

Oversewing or overcasting is used to neaten raw edges (see hand-finished seam, page 148) and join fabrics, such as on the pleated lampshade on page 108).

Work even stitches diagonally, wrapping the thread around the edges of the fabric.

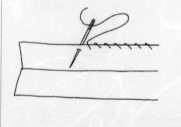

MACHINE STITCHING

STAYSTITCHING

This is a straight machine stitch used around curved and angled edges, such as necklines, to prevent stretching when handling before joining pieces together.

The stitching is done ⅛in (3mm) inside the seam line. The stitches do not need to be removed, as they will be hidden inside the finished garment between the seam allowance and the edge.

ZIG-ZAG STITCH

Zig-zag stitch is available on most sewing machines, though the very old machines often only do straight stitching. Zig-zag can be used as a decorative stitch with a contrasting thread, or for finishing raw edges and, by adjusting the length and width of the stitch, is useful for making neat buttonholes.

TOPSTITCHING

This is a line of straight machine stitching worked on the right side of the fabric, parallel to seams and edges. It is used as both a decorative and functional stitch.

Darts, Tucks & Gathering

The shape and fullness of a garment
can be controlled by means of darts,
tucks or gathering.

DARTS

Darts create shaping by controlling the fullness in the fabric to fit the garment smoothly over the contours of the figure.

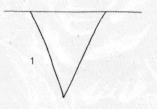 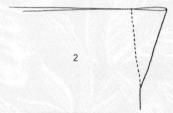

1 Before removing the paper pattern from the cut-out fabric piece, make small holes in the pattern paper at the pointed end and along the lines of the darts, then mark the position of the dart on the fabric with a tailor's chalk pencil.

2 With right sides together, fold the centre of the dart, matching the lines on each side. Stitch carefully from the wide end, tapering off to the point.

Vertical darts should be pressed towards the centre front or centre back and horizontal darts should be pressed towards the hem of the garment.

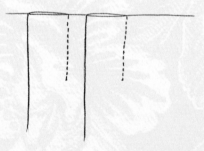

TUCKS

A tuck is a fold in the fabric that is stitched through both thicknesses. To control fullness, tucks are formed on the inside of the garment and the stitching is worked just a short way down to allow the remaining fabric to fall freely in soft pleats. Make sure you fold the fabric so that the lines match and stitch carefully to the required length.

GATHERING

Gathering is a simple method to adjust fullness in the fabric. Used widely on skirts, sleeves and frills, the gathers should be spread evenly across the material.

GATHERING BY HAND

Two straight rows of running stitches are used to gather fabric by hand. Tacking thread can be used, as the stitches are temporary and will be removed after the seam is permanently stitched.

1   Sew a few stitches over each other to secure the thread, then work a row of running stitches across the seam line of the section to be gathered, leaving a free length of thread at the end. Work another row of stitches in the same way ¼in (6mm) from the seam line.

2   Pull the two threads together to gather the section, drawing it up to fit the required measurement. Insert a pin in the fabric and secure the threads by winding them around it in a figure of eight.

3   Pin the gathered edge to the piece to be joined, matching notches, any seams and relevant markings. Adjust the gathers so that they are even between the pins. Remove the gathering stitches only after the seams have been permanently stitched.

1

2

3

GATHERING BY MACHINE

A straight stitch is used for gathering by machine. The sewing machine should be set to the longest stitch, so that the stitches are easy to gather and remove at the end.

1   Set the stitch length on the machine to a long stitch. Sew along the seam line of the section to be gathered, leaving a free length of thread at each end. Work another row of stitches in the same way ¼in (6mm) from the seam line.

2   Pull the two rows of bobbin threads (the threads that lie under the fabric) to gather one half of the section. Secure the threads by winding them in a figure of eight around a pin. Repeat for the other side to fit the required measurement.

3   Pin the gathered edge to the corresponding piece to be joined, matching notches and relevant markings. Adjust the gathers evenly between the pins before stitching the pieces together. Remove the gathering stitches only after the seams have been permanently stitched.

Pressing

Pressing the projects as you progress
will help define the lines and contours
of the piece you are working on.
Press each seam, dart and tuck
as you finish stitching it.

PRESSING EQUIPMENT

Having the equipment for pressing close to hand will make it easy to use as you sew. It is important to press each seam after stitching, to enable you to work through each stage of your sewing project with less effort and to achieve a professional finish.

IRON

You can use the point of the iron to open seams.

PRESSING CLOTH

Press on the wrong side using a damp or dry cloth to protect delicate fabric. Muslin is good as it is see through and can be used in a single layer or folded to adapt to the weight of the material you are pressing.

SLEEVE BOARD

A sleeve board is useful for pressing sleeve seams and other places that will not fit on the ironing board.

SEAM ROLL

This is a long fabric-covered roll, which is used for pressing seams.

TAILOR'S HAM

These are shaped cushions that are firmly stuffed and ideal for pressing darts and curved areas.

STEAM

Steam produces the right amount of moisture to set the position of a collar or lapel and will create a flat edge or seam. Place a dry cloth over the fabric if applying the iron directly to the fabric. If the iron is being held away from the fabric when steaming, a cloth is not required.

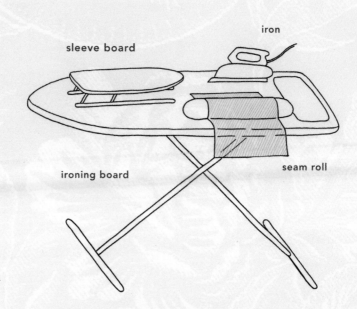

sleeve board · iron · ironing board · seam roll

PRESSING FABRICS

Pressing is not done in the same way as ironing, by dragging the iron across the fabric, but by holding the iron down on the fabric and then lifting it. Set the iron to the right temperature for the fabric (see below) and test on an odd scrap first.

SILK

Press with a medium heat, using a dry cloth to avoid the seam line marking the right side of the fabric. Using a damp cloth may cause water marks.

COTTON

A hot iron over a damp cloth will remove any creases.

LINEN

Press with a hot iron on the wrong side of the fabric.

SYNTHETICS

Use a cool iron, avoiding going over the seams as this can mark the fabric. Do not dampen the material, but pass a steam iron over the fabric without touching it with the iron.

WOOL

Use a warm iron and damp cloth. Leave on the board to dry naturally.

VELVET

Fabric with a pile should not be pressed directly. Pressing should be kept to a minimum and only done on the back of the fabric, placing the pile side down on a needle board or onto the pile side of an oddment of velvet. Velvet can be steamed, taking care not to wet the fabric. Stand the iron upright and cover it with a damp cloth. Gently pass the velvet in front of the steam to remove any wrinkles.

Finishing Touches

The attention to detail is just as
important as that given to the
construction of a hand-made project.
Personalize the piece, from the
buttonholes to the trimmings,
for a tailored finish.

BIAS BINDING

Bias binding is very versatile. It provides a neat finish as well as strengthening and concealing raw edges. It is widely available to buy with ready-pressed edges, making it simple to apply, and is available in various widths and fabrics, woven, printed and plain. However, making your own bias binding in your choice of fabric will give a professional and unique finish. Ideally, a bias strip should be cut in one long length to fit the area you wish to bind. As this is not always economical, the pieces can be joined.

MAKING YOUR OWN BIAS BINDING

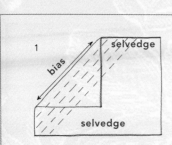

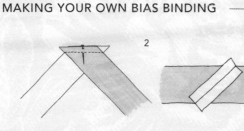

1 Find the bias of the fabric by folding it diagonally at one end. Mark the fabric with diagonal lines, parallel to the bias fold. The lines should be the desired width of your binding with an extra ¼in (6mm) each side for the seams.

2 The short ends, which are cut on the grain, will be diagonal. With right sides together, pin and stitch the short ends together and press the seam open.

3 The bias strip needs to be pressed so that it is ready to use. Fold both long edges in to the centre and press.

PIPING

Piping, a cord covered in a bias strip of fabric, is available to buy ready made. The cord can be purchased separately and is available in a range of thicknesses, so you can make your own.

MAKING PIPING

Open up the folded edges of the bias binding and wrap around the cord. Stitch close to the cord using a zipper foot on the sewing machine.

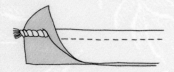

TRIMMINGS

Trimming your creation can completely change the look, adding the perfect finishing touch. Whether you want a sense of romance using delicate lace, glamour with feathers or enchantment with a sparkling beaded braid, the possibilities and range of trims are endless.

BUTTONHOLES

There are a few methods of working buttonholes; each provides a different finish to a project. Always make the buttonhole after you have chosen the buttons to ensure a perfect fit, preventing them from coming undone easily or being too tight to fasten.

BOUND BUTTONHOLE

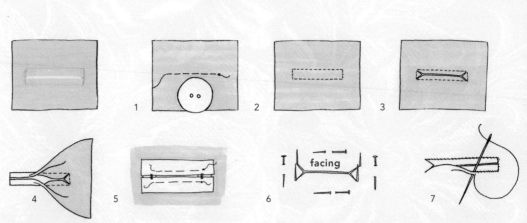

This buttonhole is neatened at the back of the work, using a facing or lining.

1   Cut a strip of fabric that is 2in (5cm) deep and 1in (2.5cm) longer than required for the buttonhole. With right sides together, place the piece of fabric on the garment and tack a line of stitches to mark the width of the button, adding an extra ¼in (6mm) at each end.

2   Work a line of stitches all around, ⅛in (3mm) above and below the line of tacking.

3   With a pair of sharp-pointed scissors, cut the opening through both thicknesses, taking care not to go through the stitches. Snip the fabric diagonally into the corners of the stitching.

4   Turn the strip of fabric to the inside. Fold the turnings down, leaving enough to cover the opening equally on each side, and tack in place.

5   With wrong side facing, fold the strip right along each long edge to form a pleat at each end to neaten. Sew the pleats to secure (see page 152).

6   Pin the facing or lining in place around the bound buttonhole. Push a pin through each corner from the right side to mark the size of the buttonhole. Cut a slit in the facing or lining to correspond with the oblong shape on the right side of the buttonhole, snipping diagonally into the corners.

7   Turn under the raw edges and hem in place. Remove the tacking stitches and press well.

WORKED BUTTONHOLE

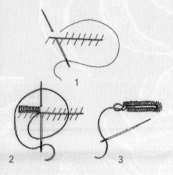

A worked buttonhole is one that is sewn by hand with a needle and thread. The position of the buttonholes should be marked out first.

1 Carefully cut the length of the buttonhole with sharp scissors. Oversew the edges to prepare for the stitching.

2 With the right side of the work facing, stitch around the oversewn edges by inserting the needle through the cut line and out to the desired length of the stitch. Keep the thread under the point of the needle and draw the needle up to tighten the thread, forming a little knot at the cut edge. Keep the stitches evenly spaced and equal in length.

3 Fan the stitches around the end towards the opening of the garment and work a straight bar of stitches at the other end to prevent the buttonhole from splitting.

MACHINE-WORKED BUTTONHOLE

This buttonhole is worked when the facings are already attached. First, mark the position of the buttonholes. Many machines have an attachment that produces the buttonhole automatically; otherwise it can be made using the zig-zag stitch. Take care to keep the lines straight and the stitches close together. At each end, the stitches should be wider than those down each side of the length. Cut the opening after stitching.

BUTTONS

Buttons are not only a decorative finishing touch, but also a practical one. There are two types of button: those with a shank and those without. The shank is a raised part underneath the button, allowing it to move freely – perfect for thicker fabric. Buttons without a shank need to be attached in such a way as to form a shank with the thread, so that it is easy to fasten and sits neatly on the fabric. Use a strong thread for sewing buttons.

SEWING BUTTONS

1 Mark the position of the button on the fabric. For horizontal buttonholes, the position of the shank should be near the end closest to the opening. For vertical buttonholes, the shank should be central.

2 Secure the thread to the fabric. Place a matchstick or hairgrip over the button and work over it when sewing the button. When the button feels secure, remove the matchstick.

3 Pull the needle through so that the thread lies between the button and the fabric. Slide the button to the top of the stitches and wind the thread around the stitches under the button to form a shank. Work some stitches through the shank and fasten off securely on the wrong side of the fabric.

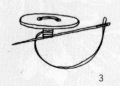

Decorating your Lingerie

Personalize your lingerie with an
embroidered motif, monogram or a lace
embellishment. Try working one design
in various embroidery stitches to create
a different effect each time.

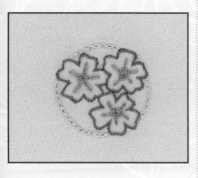

embroidered motif

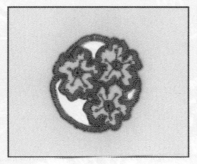

cut motif

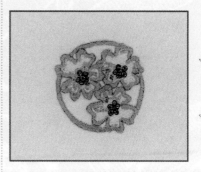

tulle-backed motif

EMBROIDERY

To embroider a motif, transfer the design (see page 169 for a template of the design shown above) by slipping dressmaker's carbon paper between the pattern and the right side of the fabric and tracing over the design. Embroider an initial (see page 169 for a template) on a pyjama pocket or front bodice, or work two interlocked letters in different shades.

embroidered initials

CUT DESIGN

To create additional detail, areas of a design that are surrounded by stitches can be cut away. Work the embroidery in buttonhole or satin stitch (see pages 164–5), and then carefully cut away the fabric at the back of the work, close to the stitches.

NET OR TULLE

Tack the net or tulle behind the fabric to be embroidered. Embroider the design through both layers of fabric. Press the work and cut away the main fabric close to the stitches to expose the net underneath. Remove the tacking stitches.

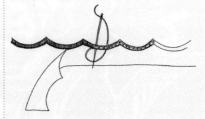

SCALLOPED EDGE

Mark out the upper and lower lines of the scallops on the right side of the fabric. Work a line of chain stitches (see page 164) in between to provide a bit of padding. Work buttonhole stitch over the chain stitch, using the lines as a guide for the needle's entry and exit points. Press the work and trim away the excess fabric.

scalloped edge

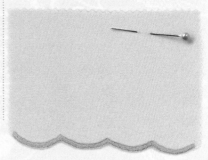

EMBROIDERY STITCHES

The following embroidery stitches are simple to work and will enable you to produce a treasured piece of needlework.

BLANKET STITCH AND BUTTONHOLE STITCH

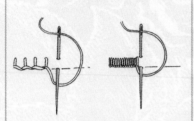

These stitches are made in the same way, the only difference being that buttonhole stitches are worked close together. On the right side of the work, insert the needle above the line of the design and bring it out on the line itself. Pass the thread under the point of the needle. Draw the needle through the loop, keeping the stitches tight but taking care not to pucker the fabric. Continue in this way, keeping the stitches the same length and evenly spaced.

CHAIN STITCH

Bring the thread through to the right side of the work at the position where the stitch is to be made and hold it down with your left thumb. Insert the needle where it first came out and bring it back through a little way from the last point, according to length of the stitch you wish to make. Pull through, keeping thread under the needle. Repeat to continue the chain.

FRENCH KNOT

1   Bring the embroidery thread through to the right side of the work at the position where the French knot is to be made and hold it down with your left thumb. Now wind the thread twice around the needle, still holding it firmly in place.

2   Insert the needle back into the work, close to the point where the thread first appeared. Pull the thread through to tighten the knot and then fasten off or bring the needle back through to the front of the work at the point where you wish to start another French knot.

1

2

STRAIGHT STITCH

This is a single stitch that can be worked in varying lengths. It is useful for embroidering short lines.

LAZY DAISY STITCH

This stitch is made in the same way as chain stitch, but the single loop is fastened with a small stitch to anchor it.

STEM STITCH

Start by making a tiny stitch. Work from left to right, bringing the needle through the outline to the centre of the stitch. Keep the stitches small and the thread below the needle. The stitches are slightly slanted and work well on curved lines.

SATIN STITCH

Work straight stitches side by side and close together across a shape. Take care to keep the stitches even and the edge neat. The finished result will look like satin.

LACE

Choose a lace that will suit the fabric you are using for your project. A fine lace will look best on a lightweight material. Old remnants of lace are perfect to enhance the vintage look of the garment.

A delicate piece of lace will benefit from being backed with net before it is attached to your lingerie. Lay the lace on the net with right sides together and stitch along the top edge to join. Trim the seam; turn to the right side and press. Tack the lower edge of the lace to the net then trim away the excess net so that the edges are even.

When attaching a length of lace to decorate the hem of a slip or nightdress, extra detail can be added by looping it (see page 166).

INSERTING A LACE MOTIF

A single lace motif makes a pretty detail for adorning your lingerie. A small design can be cut from a larger piece.

1

2

1 Cut a suitable piece from the lace, leaving a little extra around the edges. Carefully tack the lace in position on the right side of the garment. Oversew (see page 152) the edges of the lace design to the fabric using tiny, neat stitches close together.

2 Remove the tacking stitches and press the work (see page 157). Cut away the excess lace and the fabric behind it, close to the stitching.

165

JOINING LACE

Shaped pieces of lace are available to buy, but you can also cut and join a length of wide lace to fit your own design.

1   Lay one piece over the other with right sides facing up. Tack the lace in position. Oversew the top layer to the one beneath, following the pattern of the lace.

2   Remove the tacking stitches and press the work. Cut away any excess lace from both layers.

LOOPING LACE

1   To make a loop in a length of lace, run a gathering stitch (see page 155) along the straight edge and draw up to curl.

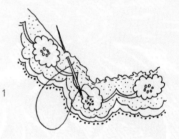

2   Tack in position and oversew the lace neatly to the fabric beneath.

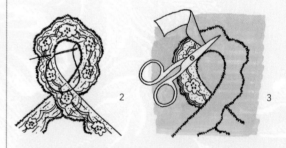

3   Remove the tacking stitches and press the work. Cut away the fabric beneath and the lace below the top layer that crosses over it.

Make Do & Mend

Vintage finds are not always in perfect
condition. With careful mending, they can
often be given a new lease of life or
transformed into an altogether new
garment or accessory.

POSSIBLE LAYOUT FOR BRA TOP

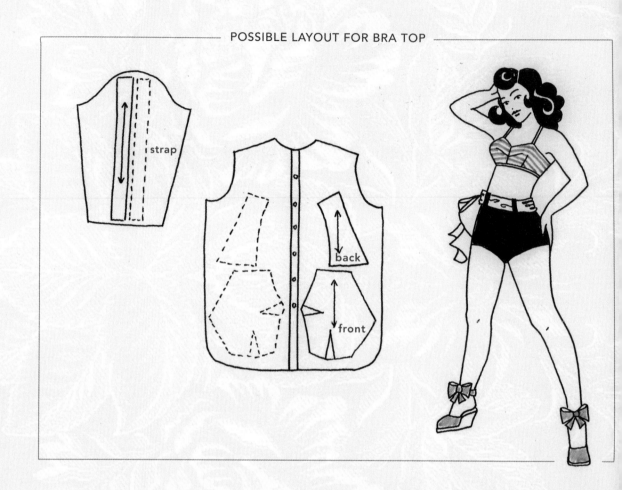

NEW FROM OLD

When a nightdress or slip has seen better days and is too worn to patch or mend, it is often only the upper part that is showing signs of wear. The lower part of the skirt can be used to make something new. With luck, you might have enough to make a pair of French knickers and a matching bra top.

Cut the worn fabric away and undo the seams. Any thin patches and tiny holes can be seen by holding the garment up to the light. These should be marked with tailor's chalk, thread or pins so that you can see which areas to avoid when cutting your pattern. Place the pattern pieces on the fabric, avoiding the thin patches and holes, rearranging them to get the best use of the material. Remember to reverse the pattern pieces when cutting multiple numbers on a single layer of fabric.

Fabrics used to make new underwear from old do not have to be limited to lingerie. On a man's vintage shirt, signs of wear and tear are often found on the collar, cuffs and elbows, leaving enough strong fabric to make a bra top, ideal for wearing on the beach! The lining can be of a contrasting fabric – a striped shirting twinned with a retro floral, for example – to create a reversible garment.

TEMPLATES

Trace the chosen template onto tracing paper, or enlarge to the desired size on a photocopier. Slip dressmaker's carbon paper, carbon side down, between the template and the right side of the fabric and trace over with a pencil to transfer the design.

MONOGRAM
See page 163

EMBROIDERY MOTIF
See page 163

PYJAMA CASE FLOWERS (ENLARGE BY 400%, USING 2 SHEETS OF A3)
See page 35

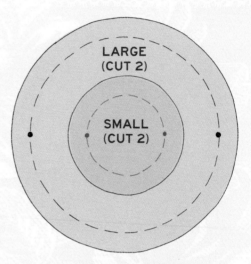

LARGE
(CUT 2)

SMALL
(CUT 2)

POWDER PUFFS (ENLARGE BY 300%)
See page 13

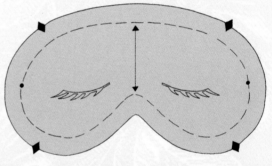

SLEEP MASK (ENLARGE BY 320%)
See page 127

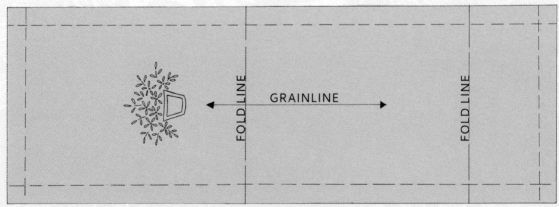

FOLD LINE

GRAINLINE

FOLD LINE

HOSIERY SACHET (ENLARGE BY 320%, TAPING TOGETHER 2 SHEETS OF A3)
See page 53

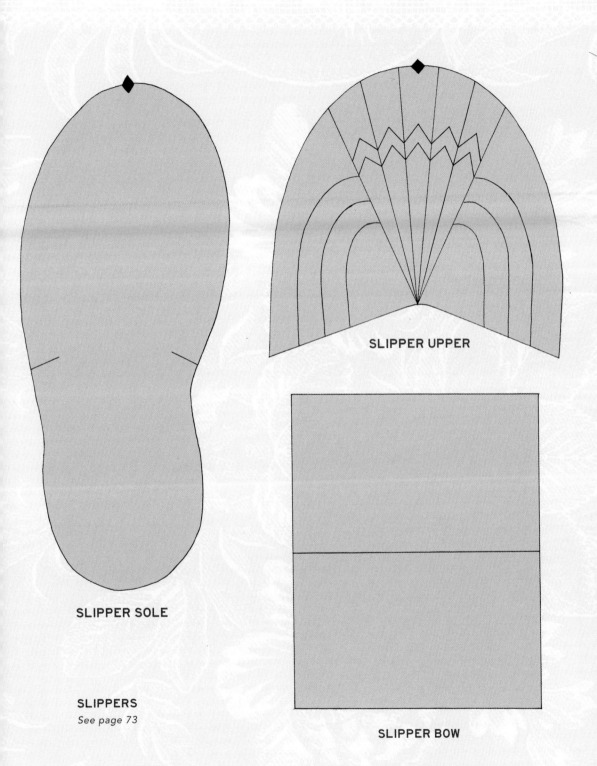

SLIPPER UPPER

SLIPPER SOLE

SLIPPERS

See page 73

SLIPPER BOW

RESOURCES

FABRIC

AUSTRALIA

FUNKY FABRIX
Shop 4/12 Blackwood Street
Mitchelton
Queensland 4053
Tel: +61 (0)421 509 502
Email: mail@funkyfabrix.com.au
www.funkyfabrix.com.au

TESSUTI FABRICS
110 Commonwealth Street
Surrey Hills
Tel: +61 (0)292 115 536
20/369 Victoria Avenue
Chatswood
Tel: +61 (0)294 153 357
141 Flinders Lane
Melbourne City
Tel: +61 (0)396 544 566
Email: fabrics@tessuti.com.au
www.tessuti.com.au

UK

BECKFORD SILK LIMITED
Beckford
Nr Tewksbury
Gloucestershire GL20 7AU
Tel: +44 (0)1386 881507
Email: sales@beckfordsilk.co.uk
www.beckfordsilk.co.uk

**THE BERWICK STREET
CLOTH SHOP**
14 Berwick Street
London W1F 0PP
Tel: +44 (0)20 7287 2881
Email: sales@theberwickstreet
clothshop.com
www.theberwickstreetclothshop.com

DITTO FABRICS
21 Kensington Gardens
Brighton
East Sussex BN1 4AL
Tel: +44 (0)1273 958959
Email: sales@dittofabrics.co.uk
www.dittofabrics.co.uk

MACCULLOCH AND WALLIS
25-26 Dering Street
London W1S 1AT
Tel: +44 (0)20 7629 0311
Email: info@macculloch.com
www.macculloch-wallis.co.uk

USA

SPOONFLOWER
Tel: +1 919 886 7885
www.spoonflower.com

THAI SILKS
252 State Street
Los Altos, California
94022
Tel: +1 800 722 7455
Email: silks@thaisilks.com
www.thaisilks.com

EMBROIDERY THREADS

FRANCE

RENAISSANCE DYEING
Andie Luijk
Le Fort
09300, Lieurac
Ariège
Tel: +33 (0)561 052760
www.renaissancedyeing.com

UK

APPLETON BROTHERS LTD
Thames Works
Church Street
Chiswick W4 2PE
Tel: +44 (0)20 8994 0711
www.embroiderywool.co.uk

COATS CRAFTS UK
Green Lane Mill
Holmfirth
West Yorkshire HD9 2DX
Tel: +44 (0)1484 681881
Email: consumer.ccuk@coats.com
www.coatscrafts.co.uk

DMC
DMC Creative World Ltd
Unit 21 Warren Park Way
Warrens Park
Enderby
Leicester LE19 4SA
Tel: +44 (0)1162 754000
www.dmc.com

ARTIFICIAL FLOWERS

UK
ABERCORN & CO.
Tel: +44 (0)1302 810083
Email: info:abercornandco.com
www.abercornandco.com

THE SHIRLEY LEAF
AND PETAL COMPANY
58 High Street
Old Town
Hastings
East Sussex TN34 3EN
Tel: +44 (0)1424 427793

USA
TINSEL TRADING COMPANY
1 West 37th Street
New York, NY 10018
Tel: +1 212 730 1030
Email: sales@tinseltrading.com
www.tinseltrading.com

BEADS

UK
BEADS UNLIMITED
Beads Unlimited
PO Box 1
Hove
East Sussex BN3 3SG
Tel: +44 (0)1273 740777
Email: mailbox@beadsunlimited.co.uk
www.beadsunlimited.co.uk

THE BEAD SHOP
(Nottingham) LIMITED
7 Market Street
Nottingham NG1 6HY
Tel: +44 (0)1159 588903
Email: info@mailorder-beads.co.uk
www.mailorder-beads.co.uk

THE BRIGHTON BEAD SHOP
21 Sydney Street
Brighton
East Sussex BN1 4EN
Tel: +44 (0)1273 675077

KERNOWCRAFT ROCKS
& GEMS LTD
Bolingey
Perranporth
Cornwall TR6 0DH
Tel: +44 (0)1872 573888
Email: info@kernowcraft.com
www.kernowcraft.com

USA
MKBEADS
618 SW 3rd st #150
Cape Coral, FL 33991
Tel: 1 (239) 634 2232
Email: sales@mkbeads.com
www.mkbeads.com

SEWING TOOLS & HABERDASHERY

AUSTRALIA
THE BUTTON BOWER
www.thebuttonbower.com

UK
ERNEST WRIGHT
AND SON LIMITED
Endeavour Works
58 Broad Lane
Sheffield S1 4BT
Tel: +44 (0)1142 754812
Email: enquiries@ernestwright.co.uk
www.ernestwright.co.uk

FRANCES DOHERTY CERAMICS
Tel: +44 (0)1273 540446
Email: frances.doherty@gmail.com
www.etsy.com/shop/francesdoherty
www.francesdoherty.co.uk

MERCHANT & MILLS LIMITED
The Gables
3 The Rucketts
Staunton on Wye HR4 7LS
Tel: +44 (0)1981 500692
www.merchantandmills.com

RAY STITCH
99 Essex Road
London N1 2SJ
Tel: +44 (0)20 7704 1060
Email: info@raystitch.co.uk
www.raystitch.co.uk

USA
BROOKLYN GENERAL STORE
128 Union St
Brooklyn, NY 11231
Tel: +1 718 237-7753
www.brooklyngeneral.com

INDEX

To place an order, or to request a catalogue,
contact: GMC Publications Ltd
Castle Place, 166 High Street, Lewes, East Sussex,
BN7 1XU United Kingdom
Tel: +44 (0)1273 488005
www.gmcbooks.com